THE Emergence OF Mahdî

Muftî Mahmûd bin Maulânâ Sulaymân Bârdolî
Lecturer at Jâmia Islâmia Dâbhel

Translated by:
Abdullâh Moolla

Publication department
Madrasah Arabia Islâmia
Azaadville, South Africa

Jointly Published by:
Zam Zam Publishers
and
Madrasah Arabia Islamia

ZAM ZAM PUBLISHERS

Title: The Emergence of Mahdi

Translated by: Abdullâh Moolla

Publication No: A-293

Second Edition: Rajab 1432, June 2011

Pages: 200

Book Also Available in:

Azhar Academy Ltd.
54-68 Little liford lane
Manor Park London E12 5QA
Phone: 020-8911-9797

Darul-Uloom Al-Madania
182, Sobieski St, Buffalo,
NY 14212 U.S.A

Dawah Corner Bookstore (ركن الدعوة)
Al Salamah Dist. Near
Shiabi Mosque, Jeddah, Saudi Arabia
Tel: 00966 2 6989380

Gangat`s
Lusaka Zambia
P.O Box # 33319
Ph: +260-95-88-0990

Islamic Book Centre
119-121 Halliwel Road,
Bolton BI 1 3NE U.K
Tel/Fax: 01204-389080

Maktaba Daralzaman
Madinah Munawara P.O Box 901
Shara-e-Siteen, Saudi Arabia
Tel: +966 4 8366666
Fax: +966 4 8383226

Jointly Published By:

Madrasah Arabia Islamia
Publication Department
1 Azaad Avenue, Azaadville
P.O Box 9786, Azaadville 1750
South Africa
Tel : 0027 11 413 2786
Fax: 0027 11 413 2787
E-mail: darululum@webmail.co.za

Zam Zam Publishers
Urdu Bazar Karachi-Pakistan.
Ph : 0092-21-32760374
0092-21-32761671
E-mail : zamzam01@cyber.net.pk

9789695830581 07321

TRANSLITERATION KEY

أإءئ	' (a slight catch in the breath)	ك	k
ا	a	ل	l
ب	b	م	m
ت	t (has an 'h' sound at the end of a sentence)	ن	n
ث	th (as in 'thorn')	ه	h (as in 'help')
ج	j	و	w
ح	h̲	ي	y (as in 'yellow')
خ	kh ('ch' in Scottish loch)		**Vowels**
د	d (the hard 'th' in 'the')	َ ً	a (slightly softer than the 'u' in 'but'; an
ذ	dh (the soft 'th' in 'the')	ِ ٍ	i (as in 'in'); in
ر	r	ُ ٌ	u ('oo' in 'book'); un
ز	z	آ	Â (elongated a, as when you would stretch the 'a' in plastic
س	s	ُو	Û ('u' in 'glue')
ش	sh	ِي	Î in ('feet')
ص	s̲	ّ	Stress symbol, indicated by repetition of letter
ض	d̲		
ط	t̲		**Honourifics**
ظ	z̲	سبحانه وتعالى	Glorified and Most High
ع	`	ﷺ	May Allâh's blessings and peace be upon him
غ	gh (similar to the French r)	عليه السلام	May peace be upon him
ف	f	رضي الله عنه رضي الله عنهم	May Allâh be pleased with him/them
ق	q (heavy k, from the throat)	رحمة الله عليه	May the mercy of Allâh be upon him

CONTENTS

Translator's Preface 8
Foreword – Maulânâ Abû Bakr Ghâzîpûrî *dâmat barakâtuhu* 9
Foreword – Maulânâ Abd ul Alîm Fârûqî Lakhnawî *dâmat barakâtuhu* 10
Foreword – Muftî Ahmad Khânpûrî *dâmat barakâtuhu* 11
Author's Preface 13
Qiyâmah and the signs of *Qiyâmah* 16
The two types of signs of *Qiyâmah* 20
The protection of *Dîn* 21
Over what type of people will *Qiyâmah* take place and the reconciliation between the two types of Ahâdîth pertaining to it 24
Khilâfah 29
The importance of the *Khilâfah* 28
Khalîfah 29
Khilâfah ar Râshida 29
The second stage of *Khilâfah* after the *Khilâfah ar Râshida* 32
The five eras of the Muslim *ummah* 34
The Twelve *Khulafâ'* 36
Revival of *Dîn* and *Mujaddid* 39
The qualities of a *Mujaddid* 40
Emphasis upon the emergence of Hadrat Mahdî 42
Emphasis upon taking the pledge of allegiance at the hands of Hadrat Mahdî 45
Ahâdîth pertaining to the emergence of *Mahdî* 47
(1) The great number of Ahâdîth pertaining to the emergence of Hadrat Mahdî 47
(2) The acceptance of the Ahâdîth pertaining to the emergence of Hadrat Mahdî 48
(3) Clarification about the name of Hadrat Mahdî 49

(4) The narrators of the Ahâdîth pertaining to Hadrat Mahdî ﷺ. 49
(5) Ahâdîth pertaining to Hadrat Mahdî ﷺ in the *Sihâh Sittah*... 50
(6) Ahâdîth pertaining to Hadrat Mahdî ﷺ in other Hadîth books ... 50
(7) The appearance of Mahdî ﷺ in the *Sahîhayn*... 51
Hadrat `Îsâ ﷺ and Hadrat Mahdî ﷺ are two different people ... 59
The belief of the emergence of *Mahdî* ... 72
The ruling pertaining to the person who rejects the emergence of *Mahdî* ... 76
The concern of the Sahâbah ﷺ and strange glad-tidings from Rasûlullâh ﷺ ... 77
The status of *Mahdî* in religion, this world, and the hereafter... 79
Remaining hidden until his emergence ... 82
When will the *Mahdî* emerge? ... 84
The general condition of the *ummah* when the time of his emergence is close ... 85
Biographic details of the *Mahdî* ... 88
Name and Lineage ... 88
Title ... 91
The word *'Imâm'* or *' `Alayhi as Salâm'* together with the name of *Mahdî* ... 92
The word *'Imâm'* ... 92
The word *'`Alayhi as Salâm'* ... 93
Place of Origin ... 95
Physical Features ... 96
The emergence of *Mahdî* and general conditions of that era and how will the emergence of the *Mahdî* take place? ... 99
The emergence of Sufyânî and the first clear miracle of Hadrat Mahdî ﷺ ... 103
Conquest of Shâm ... 109

Conquest of Constantinople 125
The descent of Hadrat `Îsâ عليه السلام and the demise of Hadrat Mahdî رضي الله عنه 129
The descent of Hadrat `Îsâ عليه السلام and the demise of Hadrat Mahdî رضي الله عنه and the general condition of that era 129
Demise of Hadrat Mahdî رضي الله عنه 139
Brief Biography of Hadrat `Îsâ عليه السلام 141
The most important task of Hadrat Mahdî رضي الله عنه 145
Social life during the era of the *Mahdî* 150
Important incidents 151
(1) Restrictions upon `Irâq, Egypt and Syria from the Romans and non-Arab nations 151
(2) The sudden incursion of the Romans into Syria 153
(3) The few Arabs during that era 153
(4) People will leave Madînah due to lack of desire and inclination 153
(5) The appearance of a mountain of gold 154
(6) Killing of the pure self 156
(7) Unity of the Muslims and Christians 156
(8) A bloody war during the days of Hajj 157
(9) Another war 157
Generally understood signs of the emergence of the *Mahdî* .. 159
(1) The rising of a sign together with the sun 159
(2) Khurâsân and the black flags 160
Scrutiny of famous signs and their rejection 164
(1) A solar and lunar eclipse in Ramadân before the emergence of the *Mahdî* 164
(2) Will there be a call from the heavens upon the emergence of Hadrat Mahdî رضي الله عنه? 168
Untraceable aspects 170

Kashf and *Ilhâm* and their status in the *sharî`ah* 173

The companions of H̲adrat Mahdî ﷺ 178

Special discussions concerning the companions of H̲adrat
Mahdî ﷺ in the Ah̲âdîth 180

Answer to an important question 181

Parts of the interview with H̲adrat Muftî Muh̲ammad Rafî
Uthmânî *dâmat barakâtuhu* 181

A worthy action of Maulâna Rafîud Dîn 188

The bequest of H̲adrat Abû Hurayrah ﷺ 189

Duâ' 191

Bibliography 192

TRANSLATOR'S PREFACE

نحمده ونصلي على رسوله الكريم

The book before you is a masterpiece. It is a collection of in-depth research and fulfills a great need. Upon meeting the author during his visit to South Africa, I was told that it was written in order to clarify the belief regarding Ḥaḍrat Mahdî ⬧, since seeing that a lot of incorrect information is easily available on the internet and through other sources. Many have fallen and many are falling into believing many strange things regarding Hadrat Mahdî ⬧.

In order to increase the readership and popularity of this book, I have tried to the best of my ability to translate simply and make the book as reader friendly as possible. For this reason, certain places have not been translated word-for-word; rather the intended meaning has been presented. Many Urdu and Arabic words cannot be translated. These have been explained in the footnotes. Similarly, we have presented an explanation or definition of the technical words throughout the book. (The author personally granted me permission to do this.) In addition, we have made certain minor additions in the text to ease the flow of language. Footnotes added by the translator or additions in the text have been indicated by the sign [T], i.e. translator. May Allâh ⬧, in His infinite mercy and grace accept this translation and make it a means of success and salvation. Âmîn

Abdullâh Moolla
Madrasah ʿArabia Islâmia, Azaadville
19 Shawwâl 1431, 28 September 2010

FOREWORD

Maulânâ Abû Bakr Ghâzîpûrî *dâmat barakâtuhu*
Editor of the Monthly Zam Zam

Maulânâ Muftî Mahmûd Hâfizjî is a capable, knowledgeable young graduate and teacher. He has great enthusiasm for knowledge, and his gaze is focused on the delicate matters of the time. Refuting the deviated sects is his specialty. He believes it his responsibility to defend truth and he fulfils it too.

Let alone the masses, very few among the elite possess correct information with regards to Hadrat[1] Mahdî. Understanding the pressing need, Muftî Mahmûd has presented authentic and verifiable information about Hadrat Mahdî - who is one of the signs of *Qiyâmah*. This enthusiasm and fervour prompted him to compile the book before you.

All praise is due to Allâh for Muftî Mahmûd has collected a lot of information about Hadrat Mahdî in this book. Generally, the masses are unaware of this. Allâh willing, this book will serve to add to their knowledge. May Allâh accept his effort.

Muhammad Abû Bakr Ghâzîpûrî

---

[1] Hadrat is an Urdu term used before the name of a luminary, whether a nabî, a sahâbî, a scholar or pious person. It is translated as 'dignified', 'superior', etc. It has been left untranslated because it generates more respect and honour for the person it refers to. It is used mainly in Urdu works and is used throughout this book as well. – [T]

FOREWORD

Hadrat Maulânâ ʿAbdul ʿAlîm Fârûqî Lakhnawî *dâmat barakâtuhu,* Son of Imâm Ahl us Sunnah

Muslims believe in the appearance of *Mahdî* based upon the Ahâdîth and *Âthâr*[2] narrated in this regard. The scholars of before clarified this reality which is not hidden from the scholarly class.

Today, opinions are expressed in various ways regarding this belief and accepted reality. This is not appropriate at all and cannot be regarded as service unto *dîn*[3].

The honourable Hadrat Maulânâ Muftî Mahmûd Bârdolî (May Allâh protect him) has clarified this matter with great caution in the book before you. This service unto knowledge and *dîn* is worthy of appreciation. There will be great benefit for the *ʿulemâ'* and the masses in the study of this book.

We make *duʿâ'* that Allâh keeps the honourable Muftî well and may He bless him with more divine ability.

ʿAbdul ʿAlîm Fârûqî
23 September 2004

---

[2] Plural of *Athar*. Majority of the scholars of Hadîth define *Athar* as *'that which is narrated from Rasûlullâh ﷺ, or the sahâbah ؓ or the tâbiʿîn, whether in marfûʿ or mauqûf form.'* According to the jurists of Khurâsân, *Athar* only refers to *mauqûf* narrations. [Irshâd Usûl ul Hadîth p.38] (The definitions of *marfuʿ* and *mauqûf* will be presented in the ensuing footnotes.) - [T]

[3] Translated as 'religion'. Islâm encourages honour and respect for every part of it. Therefore, when discussing religious matters, the Arabic word is used most of the time. – [T]

FOREWORD

Muftî Ahmad Khânpûrî *dâmat barakâtuhu*
Head Muftî of Jâmi'a Dabhel

None is aware of the actual time of occurrence of *Qiyâmah* except Allâh ﷻ. It is narrated in *Hadîth e Jibrîl*[4] that Hadrat Jibrîl عليه السلام asked Nabî ﷺ, "When will *Qiyâmah* occur?" Nabî ﷺ replied, "The questioned about it is no more knowledgeable than the questioner."

The meaning of this is that I am unaware of the correct time just as you are. However, there are various signs of *Qiyâmah* that have been explained in the Qur'ân and Hadîth. These have been classified into two categories by the *'ulemâ'*, namely, *'alâmât e sughrâ* (the minor signs) and *'alâmât e kubrâ* (the major signs). The appearance of the *Mahdî* is explained to be the first of the major signs.

In Arabic, *Mahdî* refers to someone who is guided. Considering this meaning, there has been many and will be many who would be titled *Mahdî*. The *Mahdî* that is discussed concerning *Qiyâmah* is a special individual. A lot of detail about this *Mahdî* is found in different Ahâdîth. Consequently, scholars have been lifting their pens, writing about this promised *Mahdî* from a long time already. As *Qiyâmah* approaches and Muslims on an international level undergo different tests and calamities, naturally, the desire for the promised *Mahdî* increases. Taking this internal condition and fervour of the Muslims into consideration,

---

[4] *Hadîth e Jibrîl* is a lengthy Hadîth recorded in Sahîh Muslim and other Hadîth collections. It details an incident that took place towards the end of the life of Rasûlullâh ﷺ in which Hadrat Jibrîl عليه السلام came to Rasûlullâh ﷺ in the form of a man and posed various questions about Islâm, *îmân, ihsân and Qiyâmah.* – [T]

many people spread baseless theories about the appearance of the promised *Mahdî*. It is necessary in these conditions to inform the people of the authentic narrations regarding the promised *Mahdî*.

Consequently, Muftî Mahmûd Bârdolî (May Allâh protect him) has prepared this treatise after studying the Ahâdîth and the commentaries thereof, as well as the previous books [written – (T)] on this subject. Allâh willing, it will be of benefit, and we hope that it will prove to be a guide. May Allâh greatly accept this effort. Âmîn

Dictated by:
(Muftî) Ahmad Khânpûrî
6 Dhu al Qa'dah 1427

AUTHOR'S PREFACE

Qiyâmah is a certainty. However, we have not been informed of a specific date concerning its occurrence. Nevertheless, special signs of it have been explained clearly in the Qur'ân and H̲adîth. A major sign from amongst these is the appearance of H̲ad̲rat Mahdî رضي الله عنه. A number of Muslims are desirous of the appearance of the *Mahdî* considering the conditions that the Muslim *ummah* faces today. ʿAllâmah Safârînî رحمة الله عليه states:

أي من العلامات العظمى وهي أولها أن يظهر الإمام المقتدى الخاتم للأئمة

محمد المهدي (لوائح الأنوار البهية)

The appearance of the Imâm to be followed, Leader of Imâms, Mu<u>h</u>ammad Mahdî is the first sign from the major ones (close to *Qiyâmah*).

Also, the appearance of the *Mahdî* is a reality that there is no reason to deny it. Approximately five years ago, the members of the consultation committee of Jâmiʿa Islamia Taʿlîm ud Dîn, Dâbhel/Simlak decided to establish a department that would specialize in refuting the deviated sects. The changed name of this department is *'Ta<u>h</u>affuz e Sharî'ah'*.[5] The subject of *'I<u>h</u>tisâb e Qâdiyâniyyat'*[6] fell to the lot of the author as part of this department. From amongst the various claims made by Mirzâ Qâdiyânî is the claim of being the *Mahdî* and *Masî<u>h</u>*. When I

---

[5] 'Protection of the Sharîʿah'

[6] 'Scrutiny of Qâdiyânism'

made the students of H̲adîth write the following subject matter (backed by proof):

'Leave out *Masîh̲* and *Mahdî,* Mirzâ can never be a respected human being. Also, none of the descriptions of *Mahdî* that are explained in the Ah̲âdîth fit Mirzâ Qâdiyânî in any way whatsoever.', it came across my heart that the subject matter related to the *Mahdî* should be collected separately and be presented to the *ummah*. With this purpose in mind, an effort was made to collect all the authentic and established information about the *Mahdî*. At the same time, 'weak' information would be alluded to.

Much incorrect information has become famous and common right into our circles. For example, there will be an announcement from the sky when the *Mahdî* appears and there will be an eclipse in the month of Ramad̲ân. Effort has been made to provide authentic guidance about this as well. References from the books I have benefited from have also been provided.

Concerning the Ah̲âdîth on this subject, some people have said, 'All the clear Ah̲âdîth with regards to *Mahdî* are not authentic, and those that are authentic are not clear.' Maulânâ ʿAbdur Rah̲mân Bâwâ – an active member of *'ʿÂlamî Majlis Tahaffuz e Khatm e Nubuwwah'*, London – gifted *'ʿAqîda Zuhûr e Mahdî Ah̲âdîth kî Roshnî me'* of Muftî Nizâm ud Dîn Shâmzî Shahîd رحمة الله عليه to me. Muftî Nizâm ud Dîn Shâmzî رحمة الله عليه had collected approximately fifty Ah̲âdîth on this subject in this book. He went to great lengths in the explanation of the narrators of each H̲adîth. By means of this, the baseless reality of these statements became clear. The famous research scholar, Muftî Muh̲ammad Taqî ʿUthmânî greatly praised this book in an article published in *'Al Balâgh'* (written upon the martyrdom of Muftî

Nizâm ud Dîn Shâmzî).The author (Muftî Bardolî) has taken maximum benefit from this book concerning the Ahâdîth on this subject. I have provided the names and references of the Ahâdîth books and commentaries of the scholars of Hadîth that are quoted here. Once the manuscript of this book was prepared, I handed it to my affectionate mentors, Hadrat Maulânâ Abû Bakr Ghâzîpûrî and Hadrat Maulânâ ʿAbd al ʿAlîm Fârûqî (May Allâh bless them in their lives). They provided certain guidelines as well. Muftî Rashîd Ahmad Farîdî, Shaykh al Hadîth Maulânâ Mujtabâ Lûlât, Shaykh Talha Minyâr Makkî and my honorable brother, Muftî Asʿad Khânpûrî also improved and corrected it. My second affectionate mentor, Maulânâ Muftî Ahmad Khânpûrî also read the manuscript and wrote a foreword to it as well. Maulânâ Hafiz Qârî Al Hâj Fârûqî Bambawî also strove in every way in the preparation of this book. May Allâh ﷻ reward them with the best of rewards.

A table, referencing the Ahâdîth quoted here has been placed at the end of the book. (This has been left out in this translation) – [T] This is to facilitate more research on this subject. Finally, I place my scholarly weakness and my limited knowledge of the Urdu language before the readers, due to which, many mistakes would be found. It is hoped that the readers will inform us of these so that they can be corrected in future editions.

May Allâh save me from the evil of my shallow intentions and bad deeds, and may He bless this book with acceptance.

وآخر دعوانا أن الحمد لله رب العلمين

Mahmûd bin Maulânâ Sulaymân Hâfizjî, Bârdolî
Jâmiʿa Islamia Taʿlîm ud Dîn, Dâbhel/Simlak, Gujarât

بسم الله الرحمن الرحيم

QIYÂMAH AND THE SIGNS OF *QIYÂMAH*

The advent of *Qiyâmah* is a certainty. Many people throughout the world believe and accept the concept of *Qiyâmah* in some form or the other. For us Muslims, the advent of *Qiyâmah* is a very important belief from amongst the foundational beliefs. However, knowledge of the specific time at which *Qiyâmah* will come to pass lies solely with Allâh ﷻ. In *Sûrah Luqmân* Allâh ﷻ states,

إِنَّ اللهَ عِندَهُ عِلْمُ السَّاعَةِ

Verily the knowledge of (when) Qiyâmah (will come) is only with Allâh. [Sûrah Luqmân 31:34]

In *Sûrah al A'râf* (the High Wall), Allâh ﷻ states,

يَسْأَلُونَكَ عَنِ السَّاعَةِ أَيَّانَ مُرْسَاهَا قُلْ إِنَّمَا عِلْمُهَا عِندَ رَبِّي لاَ يُجَلِّيهَا لِوَقْتِهَا إِلاَّ هُوَ

They ask you (O Muhammad ﷺ) about Qiyâmah, when will it occur? Say, "The knowledge of this is with my Rabb (only Allâh knows when it will occur). Only He will make it appear in its time. [Sûrah al A'râf (the High Wall) 7: 187]

The *Quraysh* of Makkah Mukarramah used to ask Rasûlullâh ﷺ concerning *Qiyâmah*, sometimes using family ties (as a pretext to get a convincing reply), and sometimes using the question of *Qiyâmah* as a yardstick of his *nubuwwah*. They asked, "If you are truly a messenger, then why do you not inform us of which year and which date will *Qiyâmah* occur?" However, every time they received the same reply that, the knowledge of it lies solely with my *Rabb*. No angel or messenger was given knowledge about it. Ibn Kathîr رحمة الله عليه writes in clarification of this,

أى ليس علمها إليك ، ولا إلى أحد من الخلق ، بل مردها ومرجعها إلى الله عز وجل ، فهو الذي يعلم وقتها على التعيين . تفسير إبن كثير ٤/٤٢٥

'The knowledge of *Qiyâmah* lies not with you, nor with any of the creation. The knowledge of it is with Allâh. He alone is aware of it and its precise time.'[7]

The Noble Qur'ân has explained this reality with just this much clarity. Despite this, many people involve themselves in researching the time of the advent of *Qiyâmah*. They mix *Isrâ'îlî*[8] and other narrations, and spend their entire worldly existence in the futile effort of researching and specifying the time of *Qiyâmah*. This is useless and to no avail. Allâh ﷻ further admonished such people,

لاَ تَأْتِيكُمْ إِلاَّ بَغْتَةً

(It) will appear suddenly. [Sûrah al A'râf (the High Wall) 7: 187]

---

[7] Tafsîr Ibn Kathîr vol.4 p.425

[8] In the exegesis of certain Qur'ânic verses we find statements of Jews and Christians regarding their history and explanation of certain events. We have been commanded by Rasûlullâh ﷺ not to verify them or to belie them, but to believe in what Allâh ﷻ and His Messenger ﷺ have told us. – [T]

It will come upon you in such a manner that none will have the slightest thought of it.

عن أبي هريرة رضي الله عنه أن رسول الله صلى الله عليه وسلم قال : لا تقوم الساعة حتى تطلع الشمس من مغربها ، فإذا طلعت ورآها الناس آمنوا أجمعون ، فذلك لا ينفع نفسا إيمانها لم تكن آمنت من قبل أو كسبت في إيمانها خيرا . ولتقومن الساعة وقد نشر الرجلان ثوبهما بينهما فلا يتبايعانه ولا يطويانه ، ولتقومن الساعة وقد انصرف الرجل بلبن لقحته فلا يطعمه ، ولتقومن الساعة وهو يليط حوضه فلا يسقي فيه ، ولتقومن الساعة وقد رفع أكلته إلى فيه فلا يطعمها . صحيح البخاري ٢/٩٦٣

Hadrat Abû Hurayrah ﷺ narrates that Rasûlullâh ﷺ said, "Qiyâmah will not occur until the sun rises from the west. When the sun rises from the west and the people will see it, they will all believe. However, it will be that time in which the belief (îmân) of none will be accepted. Qiyâmah will come upon you so suddenly that two people will be involved in the sale of material. They will not be able to complete the transaction nor will they be able to fold the material. Qiyâmah will come upon you so suddenly that a person will take up his utensil of his animal's milk but he will not be able to drink it. Qiyâmah will come upon you so suddenly that a person will be cleaning his pond for water but he will not be able to use it. Qiyâmah will come upon you so suddenly that a person will lift up a morsel to eat but he will not be able to eat it."[9]

In summary, the knowledge of the precise moment of *Qiyâmah* lies with Allâh ﷻ alone. However, Allâh ﷻ has informed us of many signs through His truthful messenger. Our belief is that the word of Allâh ﷻ is definite, and whatever Allâh ﷻ has informed us will undoubtedly happen. This system of the universe is subservient to the command of Allâh ﷻ. It is for this reason that before *Qiyâmah,* the world will change according to what we have been told in the Qur'ân and H̲adîth. Allâh ﷻ states,

لاَ تَبْدِيلَ لِكَلِمَاتِ اللهِ

There is nothing that can change the words (decrees and promises) of Allâh. [Sûrah Yûnus 10:64]

Therefore, the occurrence of all the signs of *Qiyâmah* that have been explained is definite. Many of them have already happened. Some are happening and many others will occur on their respective times.

It must be noted that information with regards to the signs of *Qiyâmah* is found in the books of H̲adîth under the chapter, *'Kîtab al Fitan wa Ashrâtus Sâ'a'*. They should be referenced. *'An Nihayah'* (with marginal notes and cross references) of Ibn Kathîr is available in Arabic. Similarly, *'Al Ishâ'a li Ashrât As Sâ'a'* of Sayyed Ah̲mad (in Arabic) is at our disposal. We should also study *''Asr e H̲âdir H̲adîth e Nabawî kî Roshnî me'* and *''Alâmât e Qiyâmat'* of Shâh Rafî' ud Dîn Dehlawî, both in Urdu.

---

[9] S̲ah̲îh̲ al Bukhârî vol.2 p.963

THE SIGNS OF QIYÂMAH

There are two types of signs that are explained in the Qur'ân and Hadîth:

1. 'Alâmât e Sughrâ (The Minor Signs)
2. 'Alâmât e Kubrâ (The Major Signs)

1. 'Alâmât e Sughrâ (The Minor Signs)

They can also be called 'Alâmât e Ba'îda (The Far Signs). These signs will appear before Qiyâmah, but it is not necessary that after their appearance Qiyâmah will occur soon thereafter.

2. 'Alâmât e Kubrâ (The Major Signs)

They can also be called 'Alâmât e Qarîba (The Close Signs). These signs will appear close to the advent of Qiyâmah in conflict with normal occurrences. It will become clear upon witnessing these signs that Qiyâmah is not far away.[10] The emergence of Hadrat Mahdî 🕮 is from among the major signs of this second type.

The emergence of Hadrat Mahdî 🕮 is a definite certainty. His 🕮 emergence will be a cause for advancement and prosperity in the Muslim ummah. He will fulfill major tasks after his emergence. They include the protection of dîn, the spreading of dîn, the restoration of dîn and the revival of dîn. The ummah would have been involved in these activities from before, but due to the prevalent conditions, weakness would have set in. He 🕮 will serve to remove this weakness, set these particular tasks in motion, and take them forward.

---

[10] As understood from Fath al Bârî vol.11 p.428

THE PROTECTION OF *DÎN*

The purpose of creating this world is to recognize Allâh, practice upon those things that please Him, and attain success in this world as well as the hereafter by means of it. Allâh ﷻ sent a number of messengers to this world in order to fulfill this purpose. Every messenger conveyed the message of Allâh ﷻ to His servants in their respective eras. They left this world after fulfilling their duties.

The laws that were given to the messengers of before applied to certain times and certain places only. Finally, Allâh ﷻ sent the final messenger, Hadrat Muhammad ﷺ. The *dîn* that Allâh ﷻ sent with His final messenger is a comprehensive mode of action, a complete law of life and a *dîn* never to be abrogated.

Once the Qur'ân has been declared to be the final message of Allâh ﷻ, then the demand of its eternity and universality is that it remain protected so that every man and *jinn* until the day of *Qiyâmah* can derive benefit from it. For this reason, Allâh ﷻ has taken up the responsibility of protecting the Qur'ân. Allâh ﷻ explains thus,

إِنَّا نَحْنُ نَزَّلْنَا الذِّكْرَ وَإِنَّا لَهُ لَحَافِظُونَ

Without doubt only We have revealed the Reminder (the Qur'ân) and (by various means) We shall certainly be its protectors (ensuring that it remains unchanged throughout time). [Sûrah al Hijr 15:9]

'Qur'ân' refers not only to the words. Rather, it implies both word and meaning. Due to this, the promise of protection from every form of alteration and its responsibility stands for the meaning and subject matter of the Qur'ân just as it does for the words. By protection, both knowledge and practice is meant. Correct practice will remain protected just as correct knowledge will remain protected. This is among the specialties of only the Qur'ân. The responsibility of protecting the other heavenly books was given over to those upon whom it was revealed. Allâh ﷻ states with regard to this,

بِمَا اسْتُحْفِظُواْ مِن كِتَابِ اللهِ وَكَانُواْ عَلَيْهِ شُهَدَاء

Because they were instructed to preserve Allâh's book and they were witnesses to it. [Sûrah al Mâ'idah (the Set Table) 5:44]

As long as the *ahbâr*[11] fulfilled their responsibility of protecting the *Taurâh,* the *Taurâh* remained protected. Once it fell into the hands of those who worshipped the world, it was interpolated and destroyed.

The summary of this discussion is that the words, meanings, and purport of the Qur'ân is divinely protected. It will not be deleted by anybody's deletion, it will not be suppressed by anybody's suppression, it will not become worthless on the basis of somebody's objections, and its call will not be stopped by anybody trying to stop it.

Due to the grace of Allâh ﷻ, there will always be a vast group of people in every era that will be practicing upon the *sharî'ah*. They will become embodiments of this formidable *dîn* and will fulfill the task of its protection and spread in every era.

[11] A title of the Jewish scholars, also used in the Qur'ân. – [T]

The following Hadîth explains this,

لا تزال طائفة من امتي قائمة بأمر الله ، لا يضرهم مـن خـذلهم أو خـالفهم ، حتى يأتى أمر الله وهم ظاهرون على الناس . صحيح مسلم ٢/١٤٣

There will always remain a group from amongst my ummah who will be established upon the command of Allâh. They will not be harmed by those who abandon them, or by those who are against them. This group will remain such until the command of Allâh happens.[12]

Another narration states as follows,

لا تزال طائفة من أمتي منصورين على الحق ، لا يضرهم من خذلهم حتى تقوم الساعة . جامع الترمذي ٢/٤٣

There will always be a group from my ummah that will be aided upon the truth. Those who abandon them will not harm them. (This) will remain until Qiyâmah.[13]

Therefore, there will always be a group from this *ummah* who will strive to raise the truth, and the leader of this group in its particular time will be Hadrat Mahdî ﵁.

---

[12] Sahîh Muslim vol.2 p.143

[13] Jâmi' at Tirmidhî vol.2 p.43

OVER WHAT TYPE OF PEOPLE WILL *QIYÂMAH* TAKE PLACE AND THE RECONCILIATION BETWEEN THE TWO TYPES OF A<u>H</u>ÂDÎTH PERTAINING TO IT

We come to understand from the two narrations above that there will always be a group of the pious servants of Allâh until *Qiyâmah,* and they will be occupied in the great objective of raising the word of Allâh ﷻ. However, a narration of *Sa<u>h</u>î<u>h</u> Muslim* states the following,

لا تقوم الساعة حتى لا يقال في الأرض ألله ألله

Qiyâmah will not happen until 'Allâh, Allâh' will not be said on earth.

Similarly,

لا تقوم الساعة على أحد يقول : ألله ألله . صحيح مسلم ١/٨٤

Qiyâmah will not happen upon any person who says, 'Allâh, Allâh'.

And,

ولا تقوم الساعة إلا على شرار الناس . إبن ماجة ٣٠٢

Qiyâmah will not happen except upon the worst of people.[14]

From these narrations, we come to understand that *Qiyâmah* will happen upon the worst of people. Pious people will not be in existence at that time.

The apparent contradiction between the two types of narrations can be explained in this way that words like 'until the Day of *Qiyâmah*' and 'until *Qiyâmah* happens' does not refer to the Day of *Qiyâmah* per se. It refers to a major sign of *Qiyâmah,*

---

[14] Sunan Ibn Mâjah p.302

i.e. the descent of Hadrat ʽÎsâ ﷺ. If this meaning is considered, then we come to know that this group will always remain on earth until the descent of Hadrat ʽÎsâ ﷺ. After the descent of Hadrat ʽÎsâ ﷺ, these people will gradually pass away and *Qiyâmah* will happen upon the worst of people.[15]

KHILÂFAH

عن سعيد بن جمهان رحمه الله قال : حدثني سفينة رضي الله عنه قال : قال رسول الله صلى الله عليه وسلم : الخلافة في أمتي ثلاثون سنة ، ثم ملك بعد ذلك ، ثم قال لي سفينة : أمسك خلافة أبي بكر ثم قال : وخلافة عمر وخلافة عثمان ثم قال : أمسك خلافة علي ، فوجدناها ثلثين سنة . قال سعيد : فقلت له : إن بني أمية يزعمون "أن الخلافة فيهم" قال : كذبوا بنو الزرقاء ، بل هم ملوك من شر الملوك . جامع الترمذي ٢/٤٦

It is narrated from Sa ʽîd bin Jamhân رحمه الله that he said, "Safîna ﷺ narrated to me. He said, "Rasûlullâh ﷺ said," Khilâfah will remain in my ummah for thirty years. After that, there will be kingdom." Safîna ﷺ then said to me, "Calculate the period of the khilâfah of Abû Bakr, then the khilâfah of ʽUmar, ʽUthmân and ʽAlî." We found it to be thirty years. I then said to Safîna, "The Banû Umayyah claim that the

---

[15] Refer to Nawâdir al Fiqh vol.1 p.132-133 for further clarification

khilâfah lies with them[16]*." Safîna ﷺ replied, "Banû Zurqâ has lied. They are the worst of kings."*[17]

Hadrat Maulânâ Rashîd Ahmad Gangohî رحمه الله writes in the commentary of this Hadîth,

أى : الخلافة المرضية إنما هى للذين صدقوا الإسلام بأعمالهم وتمسكوا بسنة النبي صلى الله عليه وسلم . حواشي الكوكب الدري ٢/٥٥ وحواشي على جامع الترمذي ٢/٤٦ وهكذا في مجمع بحار الأنوار ٢/٩٢

The prized *khilâfah* is the one that is established by those who attested to Islâm by way of action, and those who firmly held onto the *Sunnah.*[18]

Hadrat 'Umar ﷺ states that Rasûlullâh ﷺ said, "There will be nubuwwah and mercy for a specific time. Then there will be khilâfah and mercy for a specific time."

The words, *'Khilâfah upon the nature of nubuwwah'* appear in other narrations.[19]

Hadrat Muhammad ﷺ is the final messenger of Allâh ﷻ. There is no messenger to come after him. By fulfilling the objective of his prophet hood (recital of the verses, purification of the self, and teaching of the Qur'ân and *Sunnah*) in his lifetime,

---

[16] Meaning that the *khilâfah* runs only in their family

[17] Jâmi' at Tirmidhî vol.2 p.46

[18] Marginal notes of Al Kaukab Ad Durrî vol.2 p.55, Marginal notes of Jâmi' at Tirmidhî vol.2 p.46, Majma' Bihâr al Anwâr vol.2 p.92

[19] Mustadrak Hâkim vol.4 p.520, Hadîth 8459

Rasûlullâh ﷺ presented a comprehensive *dîn* and honourable society before mankind. Together with this, he established an equitable and just governmental system that was in accordance to the pleasure of Allâh ﷻ. The personality of Rasûlullâh ﷺ enabled him to stand at the head of both *Imâmat e Sughrâ* (leading the *salâh*) and *Imâmat e Kubrâ* (government). The system of government established by Rasûlullâh ﷺ in accordance to divine revelation cannot be found in any other era.

This system of government remained in the world after the demise of Rasûlullâh ﷺ. This system is referred to as *'Khilâfah'*. The person at the head of this system is known as the *'Khalîfah'*. In reality, *Khilâfah* is that system that is in total compliance to the teachings of *nubuwwah*, it has all the characteristics of the system laid down by Rasûlullâh ﷺ, and it runs according to the way shown in the era of Rasûlullâh ﷺ.

Hadrat Shâh Walîullâh Muhaddith Dehlawî رحمة الله عليه defines *Khilâfah*:

'*Khilâfah* is that general leadership that revives religious knowledge (teaching of Qur'ân and Hadîth, lecturing and advice) using means of propagation. It establishes the fundamental components of Islâm (like the five times daily *salâh*, *jumu'ah* and the *imâmat* thereof, collection and distribution of *zakâh*, appointment of *'amilîn*, giving or accepting testimony of the *Ramadân* crescent, the laws of *Ramadân* and *Îd* that follow, the arrangements for *Hajj* etc). (The *khalîfah*) should personally (as the representative of Rasûlullâh ﷺ) enact *jihâd* and all related matters, fulfill the responsibilities of court, establish *hudûd* (mete out sentences for crimes, murders, false accusations etc. - [T]), destroy oppression and command the good and forbid evil. (Actively) fulfilling these duties is called *Khilâfah.*'[20]

Imâm Ahl us Sunnah Maulânâ ʿAbd ush Shakûr Lakhnawî رحمة الله عليه states with regards to *Khilâfah,*

'*Khilâfah* means representative. The person who sits in as a deputy and fulfills his role is called a *khalîfah.* In the terminology of the *sharîʿah, Khilâfah* refers to that kingdom that exists for the 'establishment of the *dîn* of Rasûlullâh ﷺ and enforces the laws of *dîn.*'

It is known from the above that rule is necessary for *khilâfah,* such rule that has the capacity to serve as the representative of Rasûlullâh ﷺ.

THE IMPORTANCE OF THE *KHILÂFAH*

It was very important and necessary that the *khilâfah* and *khalîfah* remained in this *ummah.* The importance of this fact can be realized from this that the delay in burial of Rasûlullâh ﷺ after his demise was because of appointing the *khalîfah.* The shrouding and burial of Rasûlullâh ﷺ only started once Hadrat Abû Bakr رضي الله عنه was appointed the *khalîfah* by the consensus of the sahâbah رضي الله عنهم. This was done in the light of the clear indications (by speech and action) of Rasûlullâh ﷺ.

Hadrat Shâh Walîullâh رحمة الله عليه explains concerning this,

'The attention of the sahâbah رضي الله عنهم was directed to the appointment of the *khalîfah* before the burial of Rasûlullâh ﷺ. Therefore, we learn that if the sahâbah رضي الله عنهم did not know of the compulsion of appointing the *khalîfah* in the light of *sharîʿah,* (and of the

---

[20] Izâlatul Khifâ' vol.1 p.19

prohibition of delaying it), then they would have definitely not given preference to it over the burial of Rasûlullâh ﷺ.'[21]

He رحمه الله also states,

'It is *fard e kifâyah* upon the Muslims to appoint such a *khalîfah* that is an embodiment of the conditions of *khilâfah*, and it will remain *fard* until *Qiyâmah*.'[22]

KHALÎFAH

A *khalîfah* is the true representative of Rasûlullâh ﷺ. He is embellished with prophetic knowledge and qualities. He also has complete understanding of the Qur'ân and Hadîth and is an embodiment of the *Sunnah*. His heart should be filled with concern for humanity just like Nabî ﷺ. It is necessary that the *khalîfah* be a Muslim, male, intelligent, mature, just, free, a speaker, listener, seer and he should also have the ability to make *ijtihâd*.[23]

KHILÂFAH AR RÂSHIDA

Hadrat Abû Bakr رضي الله عنه guided the *ummah* by taking the reins of *khilâfah* by the consensus of the *muhâjirîn* (emigrants) and *ansâr* (helpers) in very trying times. His reign as *khalîfah* lasted two years, three months and thirteen days.

---

[21] Izâlatul Khifâ' vol.1 p.21

[22] Ibid vol.1 p.19

[23] Ibid

Hadrat Abû Bakr ؓ appointed Hadrat ʿUmar ؓ as the *khalîfah* after him. His reign lasted ten years and approximately six months. Hadrat ʿUmar ؓ appointed a council - that would consult regarding the *khalîfah* - comprising of Hadrat ʿUthmân ؓ, Hadrat ʿAlî ؓ, Hadrat ʿAbdur Rahmân bin ʿAuf ؓ, Hadrat Talha ؓ, Hadrat Zubayr ؓ, and Hadrat Saʿd bin Abî Waqqâs ؓ after he was stabbed by Abu Lu'lu' - the fire worshipper - during the Fajr *salâh*.[24]

They appointed Hadrat ʿUthmân ؓ as the *khalîfah* after consultation and deliberation. The duration of the *khilâfah* of Hadrat ʿUthmân ؓ was approximately twelve years. After the rebels assassinated Hadrat ʿUthmân ؓ, Hadrat ʿAlî ؓ was made the *khalîfah* upon the insistence of the *muhajirîn* and *ansâr*. The period of his *khilâfah* was four years and nine months.

The *khilâfah* of these four luminaries remained upon the way of Rasûlullâh ﷺ and all the conditions that determine a true *khalîfah* was found in each one of them. They made the purpose of *khilâfah* apparent in the most complete form. We refer to this blessed era as the *'Khilâfah ar Râshida'*, and the four *khulafâ'* of this era are referred to as the *'Khulafâ' ar Râshidîn'*. These four *khulafâ'* fulfilled the rights of the *khilâfah,* and in so doing, established the ideal state. They did so much that work of this nature was not to be found in the history of mankind except like that done by the messengers [May peace and blessings be upon them].

A large group from among the sahâbah ؓ and the tâbiʿîn appointed Hadrat Hasan bin ʿAlî ؓ as the *khalîfah*. Hadrat Hasan ؓ held the reins of *khilâfah* for six months. Once six months were

---

[24] Al Bidâyah wa An Nihâyah vol.7 p.144

over, he stepped down from this great position saying, "Rasûlullâh ﷺ said, '*Khilâfah* will remain for thirty years after me.' The six months left for the thirty years to be completed have passed."

It was as if the *khilâfah* of Hadrat Hasan was the completion of the *khilâfah* of Hadrat ʿAlî .

قال العلماء : "لم يكن في الثلثين بعده صلى الله عليه وسلم إلا الخلفاء الأربعة وأيام الحسن" . تاريخ الخلفاء ١٠

The *ʿulemâ'* have stated, 'There is no era included in the thirty years after Rasûlullâh ﷺ except the rule of the four *khulafâ'* and Hasan .'[25]

والحسن آخر الخلفاء بنصه . تاريخ الخلفاء ١٣١

And Hasan () is clearly the last *khalîfah*.[26]

In this way, the thirty years of '*khilâfah* upon the nature of *nubuwwah*' was completed. Consequently, Maulânâ Manzûr Ahmad Nuʿmânî writes in the explanation of the following narration of Sunan Abû Dâwûd[27],

خلافة النبوة ثلاثون سنة

Khilâfah upon the nature of nubuwwah is for thirty years

'The martyrdom of Hadrat ʿAlî took place in precisely the thirtieth year after the demise of Rasûlullâh ﷺ. His elder son, Hadrat Hasan became the *khalîfah* after him. However, in order to finish off the infighting among the Muslims, he stepped down from the *khilâfah* and reconciled with Hadrat Muʿâwiyah

---

25 Târikh al Khulafâ' p.10

26 Ibid p.131

27 Chapter on the Khulafâ', p.638, Hadîth 4647

ﷺ, handing the *khilâfah* over to him. All this was in accordance to the prophesy of Rasûlullâh ﷺ.

Thirty years will be complete upon the inclusion of these few months of *khilâfah* held by Hadrat Hasan ﷺ. Hence, '*khilâfah* upon the nature of *nubuwwah*' and '*khilâfah ar râshida*' - referred to as '*khilâfah an nubuwwah*' in the Ahâdîth - remained for these thirty years. After this, changes set in the method of action and gradually monarchy tainted '*khilâfah* upon the nature of *nubuwwah*'.

This Hadîth is a miracle of Rasûlullâh ﷺ and a proof of his *nubuwwah* just like the other prophesies he had made. He ﷺ gave information about events that happened after his demise and there was no outward means of coming to know of it. It is quite apparent that he ﷺ received this knowledge from Allâh ﷻ by means of *wahî*.[28]

THE SECOND STAGE OF *KHILÂFAH* AFTER THE *KHILÂFAH AR RÂSHIDA*

Another stage of *khilâfah* began after the *khilâfah ar râshida*. It is also called monarchy or kingdom. This *khilâfah* began with the Banû Umayyah, it was carried on by the Banu ʿAbbâs and it ended due to a grand plot while held by the Ottomans in 1921. Firmness upon the method of Rasûlullâh ﷺ in this second era was not to the degree to which it was found in the era of the *khilâfah ar râshida*. The *khalîfah* and other leaders began to commit many punishable acts in the light of *sharîʿah*. In addition, many weaknesses came about in the system of government.

---

28 Maʿârif ul Hadîth vol.7 p.244

Despite this, we refer to this second era as *'Khilâfah Islâmiya'* because the Muslim lands were not converted into *Dâr al Harb* in this era. There was a religious system in place that was run for Islâm on a collective scale. The enemies were forced to think twice before turning the Muslims into a single fresh morsel, as is the case today. The *khilâfah* served to protect the *dîn* and the *sharî'ah* and it stood guard over the Muslim world. Today, we Muslims passionately perceive the importance of the *khilâfah* since it is not in existence. Considering these excellent characteristics, Rasûlullâh ﷺ also emphasized obedience to the *khulafâ'* of this era in governmental affairs so that this system is not weakened in any way. In the light of the emphatic instructions of Rasûlullâh ﷺ, the sahâbah ؓ, tâbi'în and sages humbled themselves and pledged allegiance to these rulers in governmental affairs and they did not rebel.

Hadrat Shâh Walîullâh رحمة الله عليه states,

'It is *harâm* to rebel against the ruler after he has been unanimously elected, even though all the conditions for *khilâfah* are not found in him, except in the instance where clear *kufr* is established from him.'[29]

He رحمة الله عليه further explains,

'It is necessary to execute the commands of the ruler that deal with the general benefit of the Muslims and it is not in conflict with the *sharî'ah*. It matters not whether the ruler is just or not.'[30]

This system of *khilâfah* remained for approximately thirteen centuries. This was the second stage of the *khilâfah*.

---

[29] Izâlatul Khifâ' vol.1 p.28

[30] Ibid

عن حذيفة بن اليمان رضي الله عنه قال : قال رسول الله صلى الله عليه وسلم : "إن أول دينكم نبوة ورحمة وتكون فيكم ما شاء الله أن تكون ، ثم يرفعها الله جل جلاله . ثم تكون خلافة على منهاج النبوة ما شاء أن تكون ، ثم يرفعها الله جل جلاله . ثم يكون ملكا عاضا فيكون ما شاء الله أن يكون ، ثم يرفعه الله جل جلاله . ثم تكون ملكا جبرية فتكون ما شاء الله أن تكون ، ثم يرفعه الله جل جلاله . ثم تكون خلافة على منهاج النبوة ، تعمل في الناس بسنة النبي ويلقى الإسلام بجرانه في الأرض ، يرضى عنها ساكن السماء وساكن الأرض ، لا تدع السماء من قطر الا صبته مدرارا ، ولا تدع الأرض من نباتها وبركاتها شيئا الا أخرجته." رواه أحمد في مسنده في حديث النعمان بن بشير رضي الله عنه . رقم الحديث ١٨٣٦٦ والبيهقي في دلائل النبوة .

Hadrat Hudhayfah bin Yamân ﵁ says that Rasûlullâh ﷺ said,

(1) "Your dîn began with nubuwwah and mercy. It will remain among you until Allâh wishes. Allâh will then take it away. [Consequently, Rasûlullâh ﷺ lived for sixty three years and passed away in Rabî ʿal Awwal, 11 A.H]

(2) Then khilâfah upon the nature of nubuwwah will be established. It will remain for as long as Allâh wishes, where after He will take it away [After the demise of Rasûlullâh ﷺ, the khilâfah upon the nature of nubuwwah remained for thirty years.]

(3) *Thereafter will be an era of harsh and strong kingdom. It will remain for as long as Allâh wishes, where after He will take it away [It began in 41 A.H and came to an end in 1338 A.H]*

(4) *Then an oppressive kingdom will be formed. It will remain for as long as Allâh wishes, where after He will take it away [This is the fourth kingdom after the khilâfah came to an end in 1338 A.H]*

(5) *Finally, the khilâfah ar râshida will once again return. It will be totally upon the nature of nubuwwah, and Islâm will place its neck upon the earth (Islâm will be established in the earth). The inhabitants of the earth and skies will be happy with the khilâfah of that time. Rain will fall in abundance and a lot of vegetation and blessings will come forth from the earth."*[31]

The glad-tidings of the *khilâfah* upon the nature of *nubuwwah* in the latter times mentioned in this Hadîth is also related to the era of Hadrat Mahdî رضي الله عنه.

[31] Musnad Ahmad, Dalâ'il un Nubuwwah of Bayhaqî

THE TWELVE *KHULAFÂ'*

عن جابر بن سمرة رضي الله عنه قال : قال رسول الله صلى الله عليه وسلم

"يكون من بعدي اثنا عشر أميرا " قال رضي الله عنه : ثم تكلم بشيئ لم أفهمه

، فسئلت الذي يليني فقال : قال "كلهم من قريش". هـذا حـديث حـسن

صحيح . ترمذي ٢/٤٦ أبو داؤد ٢/٥٨٨

Jâbir bin Samurah ❀ narrates that Rasûlullâh ❀ said, "There will be twelve khalîfahs after me." The narrator ❀ says, "Rasûlullâh ❀ then mentioned a few things that I did not understand. I then asked the person seated nearby. He said that Rasûlullâh ❀ said, "They will all be from the Quraysh."[32]

Another narration states,

"There is no messenger after me, however, there will be a great number of khulafâ'."

Note: These twelve could be referred to as *khulafâ'*. It is as though the meaning of *khalîfah* here is king or the head of the government.

Many interpretations have been provided for this Ḥadîth. The most preferred view is that it is not necessary for these twelve to come after Rasûlullâh ❀ in sequence. In different eras until *Qiyâmah*, this number will be completed. The author of *Badhl ul Majhûd* states,

---

[32] Jâmiʿ at Tirmidhî vol.2 p.46, Sunan Abû Dâwûd vol.2 p.588

قال البعض : المراد بهم الذين هم على سيرة الخلفاء (الراشدين) وآخرهم الامام المهدي " . بذل المجهود ١٠١/٥

Some scholars have said, 'This refers to those who will be upon the way of the *khulafâ' ar râshidîn,* the last of whom is Imâm Mahdî.'[33]

Hadrat Maulânâ Khalîl Ahmad Sahâranpûri رحمة الله عليه has given preference to this view. Similarly, Imâm Suyûti رحمة الله عليه and Shâh Walîullâh رحمة الله عليه also favour this view. This much is certain that the last of these twelve *khulafâ'* will be Hadrat Mahdî رضي الله عنه. Consequently, Imâm Abû Dâwûd رحمة الله عليه has recorded the Hadîth of the twelve *khulafâ'* in *Kitâb al Mahdî.* In doing so, he has indicated that the twelfth *khalîfah* is Hadrat Mahdî رضي الله عنه.

Note: There is another view besides all the interpretations given. It states that the twelve *khulafâ'* refer to the leaders of the Banû Umayyah that ascended the throne after Hadrat Mu'âwiyah رضي الله عنه. It is as though the Hadîth means that the power and strength of Islâm as far as government is concerned will remain during the reign of these twelve, and that kingdom will remain during this time.

The names of these twelve are as follows,

1. Yazîd bin Mu'âwiyah
2. Mu'âwiyah bin Yazîd
3. 'Abdul Malik
4. Walîd
5. Sulaymân
6. 'Umar bin 'Abdul 'Azîz
7. Yazîd bin 'Abdul Malik

[33] Badhl ul Majhûd vol.5 p.101

8. Hishâm
9. Walîd bin Yazîd
10. Yazîd bin Walîd bin ʿAbdul Malik
11. Ibrâhîm bin Walîd
12. Marwân bin Muhammad

These twelve ruled during the reign of the Banû Umayyah. After them, the kingdom fell to the lot of the Banû ʿAbbâs.

Another view concerning this is that the twelve refers to those twelve *khulafâ'* that will come after Hadrat Mahdî رضي الله عنه. Five are from the progeny of Hadrat Hasan رضي الله عنه and five from the progeny of Hadrat Husayn رضي الله عنه. After these ten, a pious person from the progeny of Hadrat Hasan رضي الله عنه will rule and his son after him. In this way, twelve are completed and all of them will be on the truth.[34]

One view is that the twelve refers to the four *khulafâ' ar râshidîn*, Hadrat Hasan رضي الله عنه, Hadrat Muʿâwiyah رضي الله عنه, Hadrat ʿAbdullâh bin Zubayr رضي الله عنه and Hadrat ʿUmar bin ʿAbdul ʿAzîz رحمة الله عليه. They total eight. Then, Hadrat Mahdî ʿAbbâsî رحمة الله عليه and Hadrat Tâhir رحمة الله عليه - who was very just. The rest are awaited. One of them is Hadrat Mahdî رضي الله عنه.[35]

Note: The most important thing to understand at this time is that these twelve *khulafâ'* are not sinless *(maʿsûm)*. They will also not be upon a status of *nubuwwah* or higher. Similarly, rule for them will not be with a special outstanding quality. Also, Muftî Yûsuf Ludhiyânwî رحمة الله عليه states with regards to the *'Ithnâ ʿAshar'* Imâms of the *shîʿa,*

---

[34] Majmaʿ Bihâr ul Anwâr vol.1 pp.82-84

[35] Târîkh ul Khulafâ' p.12

'The *Ahl us Sunnah* also believe them to be personalities to be followed, except with two differences,

1. The *shî'as* believe them to be free from sin like the messengers, make obedience to them obligatory and understand them to be commanded by Allâh. These beliefs are special with the messengers (*Ambiyâ'*) according to the *Ahl us Sunnah*.

2. The rulings attributed to them are not correct. The narrators of these rulings cannot be relied upon.[36]

REVIVAL OF *DÎN* AND *MUJADDID*

عن أبي علقمة رحمه الله ، عن أبي هريرة رضي الله عنه فيما أعلم عن رسول الله
صلى الله عليه وسلم قال : إن الله يبعث لهذه الامة على رأس كل مائة سنة مـن
يجدد لها أمر دينها . مستدرك ٤/٥٦٨ . رقم الحديث ٨٥٩٣

Abû 'Alqamah رحمه الله *narrates from Abû Hurayrah* رضي الله عنه *from that which he learnt from Rasûlullâh* ﷺ, *"Indeed Allâh will send for this ummah such a person at the turn of each century who will revive their religious matters."*[37]

The protection of Islâm until *Qiyâmah* is a hidden system from Allâh ﷻ. This is an outstanding blessing for this *ummah*. However, satanic powers will try to interpolate this religion in every era.

---

[36] Al Mahdî wal Masîh p.23
[37] Mustadrak vol.4 p.568

Harshness and extremism (positive and negative) is the foundation for the beginning of interpolation. Interpreting the *dîn* in accordance to ones desires - away from the balanced way - and to explain *dîn* by means of incorrect viewpoints and deviation are the destructive sicknesses that become the means of depriving the *ummah* of true and original *dîn*. Allâh ﷻ has greatly favoured this *ummah* by establishing this *mujaddid* chain in order to keep this powerful *dîn* pure from every form of interpolation and heresy in every era.

TAJDÎD

Faqîh ul Ummah Muftî Ma<u>h</u>mûd <u>H</u>asan Gangohî رحمة الله عليه explains the meaning of *tajdîd e dîn* (revival of religion),
'Over time, certain laws of *sharî ̔ah* were not given due attention. They were left out because of the overpowering of desires and lusts and the efforts of the carnal self and the devil. To illuminate them, turn ones attention to them and make an effort to practice upon them is referred to as *tajdîd e dîn*.'[38]

THE QUALITIES OF A *MUJADDID*

- He is a true representative of Rasûlullâh ﷺ in knowledge and practice.
- He has been given a magnetic personality by Allâh ﷻ like that of a messenger.

---

[38] Fatâwâ Ma<u>h</u>mûdiyyah vol.15 p.129

- The hearts of people are drawn towards him on account of his lineage, family, character and habits.
- Due to his great *îmânî* insight, he can diagnose the sicknesses of the *ummah* and prepare a *modus operandi* to treat them in the light of the Qur'ân and Hadîth. He then executes it.
- He rips the veil of innovations and customs.
- He revives beliefs, worship, social etiquette, business dealings, character, and system of government. In fact, he revives every facet of life.
- He is not awed by anyone in proclaiming the truth.
- Allâh ﷻ places enthusiasm in people's hearts to obey and love him.
- Those who have concern for *dîn* surround him.
- He will face much opposition just as the messengers had to. Hardship will come his way too. Due to unseen help, the cloud of difficulties will slowly fade and his rule will gain ground in the world.
- A *mujaddid* has natural complete mastery over knowledge and recognition; he also has great insight into *dîn* and the *Sunnah*.
- The quality of *taqwâ* and piety is perfect in him.
- A *mujaddid* spreads knowledge and he honours the scholars.
- Allâh ﷻ will create a special servant of His or a group in the *ummah* that possesses these qualities at the start of every century, or in every era. Hadrat Mahdî عليه السلام is the final link in the blessed *mujaddid* chain. A *mujaddid* and *faqîh* of the recent past, Hadrat Gangohî رحمة الله عليه explains,

هو آخر مجددي هذه الأمة . الكوكب الدري ٢/٥٧

Hadrat Mahdî ﷺ will be the final *mujaddid* of this *ummah.*[39]

Note: A *mujaddid* will come to know of his standing through *ilhâm* or by various signs that allude to him being a *mujaddid*. However, he will not reach the stage of *wahî*. Similarly, a *mujaddid* will be recognized because of the special work that he is involved in.[40]

EMPHASIS UPON THE EMERGENCE OF HADRAT MAHDÎ ﷺ

The emergence of Hadrat Mahdî ﷺ is greatly emphasized in the Ahâdîth. Examples of this are presented below,

عن عبد الله بن مسعود رضي الله عنه عن النبي صلى الله عليه وسلم قال : "لو لم يبق من الدنيا إلا يوم – قال : زائدة (الراوي) – لطول الله ذلك اليوم حتى يبعث رجلا مني (أو قال) من أهل بيتي ، يواطئ اسمه اسمي واسم أبيه اسم أبي – زاد في حديث فطر : يملأ الأرض قسطا وعدلا كما ملئت ظلما وجورا"

أبو داؤد ، كتاب المهدي ٥٨٨/٢

Hadrat Abû Hurayrah ﷺ narrates from Rasûlullâh ﷺ that he said, "If there was one day remaining for the existence of this world - Zâ'ida (the narrator says) – then Allâh would lengthen that day until he

---

[39] Al Kaukab Ad Durrî vol.2 p.57

[40] Summarized from Fatâwâ Mahmûdiyya vol.13 p.403

sends a person from me (or he said, from my family) such that his name will be like mine, and his father's name will be the same as my father's name. The narration of Fiṭr adds, "He will fill the earth with justice and equity just as it was filled with oppression and tyranny."[41]

Another narration is as follows,

عن أبي هريرة رضي الله عنه قال : لو لم يبق من الدنيا إلا يوما لطول الله ذلك

اليوم حتى يلى . هذا حديث حسن صحيح . ترمذي ٤٧/٢

It is narrated from Ḥaḍrat Abû Hurayrah that he said, "If there was only a single day left of the existence of the world, then Allâh would have lengthened that day until a person is made the ruler."[42]

Another narration states,

عن عبد الله بن مسعود رضي الله عنه قال : قال رسول الله صلى الله عليه وسلم

: "لا تذهب الدنيا حتى يملك العرب رجل من أهل بيتي يواطئ اسمه

اسمي". هذا حديث حسن صحيح . ترمذي ٤٧/٢

Ḥaḍrat ʿAbdullâh bin Masʿûd narrates that Rasûlullâh said, "The world will not come to an end until a person from my family is not made the ruler over Arabia. His name will be the same as mine's."[43]

'Ruler over Arabia' is mentioned in the above narration. This means that because Arabia is the centre and capital of Islâm, therefore rule over it implies rule over the entire earth. In addition, the Arabs are the most honourable nation. Hence, being a leader of the Arabs implies being the ruler over everyone.

---

[41] Sunan Abû Dâwûd vol.2 p.588
[42] Jâmiʿ at Tirmidhî vol.2 p.47
[43] Ibid

Maulânâ Manzûr Ahmad Nu'mânî رحمة الله عليه writes, 'It could also be said that initially, rule will be established in Arabia, then in the entire world, or, the capital will be Arabian.'[44]

The above-mentioned point is explained elsewhere thus,

لا تذهب الايام والليالي حتى يملك رجل من أهل بيتي ، يواطئ اسمه اسمي واسم أبيه اسم أبي ، فيملأ الأرض قسطا وعدلا كما ملئت ظلما وجورا" . مستدرك للحاكم . رقم الحديث ٨٧١٣

'Day and night will not cease to exist until a person from my family is made ruler, whose name corresponds with mine's, and his father's name corresponds with my father's name. He will fill the earth with justice and equity just as it was filled with oppression and tyranny.'[45]

"لا تقوم الساعة حتى تملأ الأرض ظلما وجورا وعدوانا ثم يخرج من أهل بيتي من يملأها قسطا وعدلا كما ملئت ظلما وعدوانا" . مستدرك . رقم الحديث ٨٦٦٩

'Qiyâmah will not happen until the earth is not filled with oppression, tyranny and enmity. A person from my family will then emerge who will fill the earth with justice and equity just as it was filled with oppression and tyranny.'[46]

It is inferred from these two narrations that night and day will not cease to exist, or, *Qiyâmah* will not come until Hadrat Mahdî رضي الله عنه does not emerge.

---

[44] Ma'ârif ul Hadîth vol.8 p.170

[45] Mustadrak Hâkim, Hadîth 8713

[46] Ibid, Hadîth 8669

The summary of these narrations is that the emergence of Hadrat Mahdî ﷺ is a certainty and a source of mercy such that it is *wâjib*[47] to believe in the emergence of Hadrat Mahdî ﷺ as will be explained later.

EMPHASIS UPON TAKING THE PLEDGE OF ALLEGIANCE AT THE HANDS OF HADRAT MAHDÎ

It is necessary for man to aid every venture of goodness and piety to the best of his ability. In accordance to the teachings of the pure *sharî'ah*, it is a demand of faith and character to help, remove obstacles, and not to hinder the path of a reformer, *mujaddid* or a person who stands up to proclaim the truth. However, great emphasis is found in the Ahâdîth to aid Hadrat Mahdî ﷺ when he emerges and to take the pledge of allegiance at his hands. Rasûlullâh ﷺ has explained with great emphasis thus,

"He who finds this time (the era of Hadrat Mahdî ﷺ) should come to him, even if he has to come crawling on ice."

Herewith explains a Hadîth,

عن عبد الله بن مسعود رضي الله عنه قال : بينما نحن عند رسول الله صلى الله

عليه وسلم إذ أقبل فتية من بني هاشم ، فلما رآهم النبي صلى الله عليه وسلم

اغرورقت عيناه وتغير لونه . قال (عبد الله) فقلت : ما نزال نرى في وجهك

شيئا نكرهه ، فقال : "إنا أهل بيت اختار الله لنا الآخرة على الدنيا ، وإن أهل

---

[47] Compulsory –[T]

بيتي سيلقون بعدي بلاء وتشريدا وتطريدا حتى يأتي قوم من قبل المشرق معهم رايات سود ، فيسئلون الخير فلا يعطونه ، فيقاتلون ، فينصرون ، فيعطون ما سئلوا ، فلا يقبلون حتى يدفعوها إلى رجل من أهل بيتي ، فيملأ قسطا كما ملئوها جورا ، فمن أدرك ذلك منهم فليأتهم ولو حبوا على الثلج .

ابن ماجة ٣٠٩

Hadrat ʿAbdullâh bin Masʿûd ﷺ narrates, "We were once sitting with Rasûlullâh ﷺ. Suddenly, a few youngsters from Banû Hâshim came to him. When he (Rasûlullâh ﷺ) saw them, his eyes became wet with tears and the colour of his face changed. I (Hadrat ʿAbdullâh bin Masʿûd ﷺ) said, "We see the effects of grief on your face which is a cause of uneasiness for us." Rasûlullâh ﷺ then said, "Indeed Allâh has preferred for us, the ahl al bayt, the hereafter over this world. The people of my household will face great difficulty, hurt and will be reviled after my demise. This will be the case until a nation that has black flags will rise from the east. They (my family) will ask good from them, but they will not be given. They will then war, and will be helped. They will be given what they ask but they will not accept, until they give to a person from my family. He will fill the earth with justice and equity just as it was filled with oppression. So, whoever finds him should go to him, even though he may have to crawl on ice."[48]

We can gauge from these blessed words the emphasis that Rasûlullâh ﷺ placed upon helping Hadrat Mahdî ﷺ and taking the pledge of allegiance upon his hands.

---

[48] Sunan Ibn Mâjah p.309

Hadrat Shâh Walîullâh رحمة الله عليه says, 'It will be *wâjib* to obey Hadrat Mahdî رضي الله عنه in the affairs related to the *khilâfah* once his era dawns.'[49]

AHÂDÎTH PERTAINING TO THE EMERGENCE OF HADRAT MAHDÎ رضي الله عنه

(1) THE GREAT NUMBER OF AHÂDÎTH PERTAINING TO THE EMERGENCE OF HADRAT MAHDÎ رضي الله عنه

Hâfiz Ibn Hajar 'Asqalânî رحمة الله عليه says that the Ahâdîth pertaining to the emergence of Hadrat Mahdî رضي الله عنه have reached the level of *tawâtur*[50]. (Shaykh Barzanji رحمة الله عليه and 'Allâmah Suyûtî رحمة الله عليه explain that *tawâtur ma'nawî*[51] is meant by this.)

Qâdî Shaukânî writes in *Al Fath Ar Rabbânî,*

وجميع ما سقناه بلغ حد التواتر ، كما لا يخفى على من له فضل اطلاع . بحوالة تحفة الأحوذي ٢٠٤/٦

'All the narrations that we have recorded have reached the level of *tawâtur* (see footnote 50). This is not hidden from those of knowledge.'

---

[49] Izâlatul Khifâ' vol.1 p.26

[50] *Tawâtur* refers to a narration that has been narrated by such a large number of people through every era that it is impossible to conceive that all of them have lied. [Irshâd Usûl ul Hadîth p.42] – [T]

[51] *Tawâtur e Ma'nawî* refers to a number of narrations whose subject matter or meaning has reached the level of *Tawâtur*. [Irshâd Usûl ul Hadîth p.44] – [T]

A similar observation has been made in *Sharh 'Aqîdah As Safârînî,*

قد كثرت الروايات بخروج المهدي ، حتى بلغت حد التواتر المعنـوي . شرح عقيدة السفاريني ٢/٨٠

'The Ahâdîth pertaining to the emergence of Hadrat Mahdî ؓ are so great in number that they have reached the level of *tawâtur ma'nawî* (see footnote 51).'

Shâh 'Abdul Haq Muhaddith Dehlawî ؒ explains in *Ashi'atul Lam'ât,*

'Many narrations in this regard have reached a level very close to *tawâtur* (see footnote 50).'[52]

(2) THE ACCEPTANCE OF THE AHÂDÎTH PERTAINING TO THE EMERGENCE OF HADRAT MAHDÎ ؓ

The entire Muslim *ummah* has accepted the Ahâdîth that explain the emergence of Hadrat Mahdî ؓ. 'Allâmah Munâwî ؒ says in *Fayd ul Qadîr,* the commentary of *Jâmi 'us Saghîr,*

أخبار المهدي كثيرة شهيرة أفردها غير واحد في التأليف الـخ . فـيض القـدير شرح جامع الصغير ٦/٢٧٩

'The Ahâdîth concerning Hadrat Mahdî ؓ have been narrated in great number, and they are famous as well. Scholars have compiled separate works only on this subject.'

---

[52] Ashi'atul Lam'ât vol.4 p.338

(3) CLARIFICATION WITH REGARDS TO THE NAME OF HADRAT MAHDÎ ﷺ

Approximately more than ninety *marfû*ʿ [53] Ahâdîth have been narrated, thirty of which clearly state the name of Hadrat Mahdî ﷺ. Besides this, (mention of his name) is also found in the Âthâr (see footnote 2) of the sahâbah ﷺ and the sayings of the tâbiʿîn.

Note: The name of Hadrat Mahdî ﷺ is not mentioned clearly in some Ahâdîth. However, according to the scholars of Hadîth, there is a principle that states that if there are different Ahâdîth narrated on one particular story, and some are concise or unclear, while others are detailed, then the detailed narrations will be considered to be the explanation of the concise or unclear narrations.

(4) THE NARRATORS OF THE AHÂDÎTH PERTAINING TO HADRAT MAHDÎ ﷺ

Approximately twenty five sahâbah ﷺ and tâbiʿîn have narrated Ahâdîth pertaining to Hadrat Mahdî ﷺ. Among them are such great personalities like, Hadrat ʿUthmân ﷺ, Hadrat ʿAlî ﷺ, Hadrat ʿAbdullâh bin Masʿûd ﷺ, Hadrat ʿAbdullâh bin ʿAbbâs ﷺ, Hadrat ʿAbdullâh bin ʿUmar ﷺ, Hadrat Abû Hurayrah ﷺ, Hadrat Talha ﷺ, Hadrat Anas ﷺ, Hadrat ʿAbdur Rahmân bin ʿAuf ﷺ and Hadrat Abû Saʿîd Khudrî ﷺ. The narrators from among the Ummahât al Mu'minîn include Hadrat Umm e Salamah *radiyallâhu anhâ* and Hadrat Umm e Habîbah *radiyallâhu anhâ.*

---

[53] *Marfû*ʿ is a narration whose chain of narration is linked directly to Rasûlullâh ﷺ. [Irshâd Usûl ul Hadîth p.53] – [T]

(5) AHÂDÎTH PERTAINING TO HADRAT MAHDÎ ؑ IN THE *SIHÂH SITTAH*[54]

From amongst the compilers of the *sihâh sittah,* Imâm Tirmidhî رحمۃ اللہ علیہ, Imâm Abû Dâwûd رحمۃ اللہ علیہ and Imâm Ibn Mâjah رحمۃ اللہ علیہ have included a separate chapter dealing solely with the subject of Hadrat Mahdî ؑ.

Note: There are certain fabricated narrations in Ibn Mâjah. However, the Ahâdîth pertaining to Hadrat Mahdî ؑ are not among them. This is explained in *'Mâ Tamassu Ilayhi al Hâjah li man Yutâli'u Ibn Mâjah'* of 'Allâmah 'Abdur Rashîd Nu'mânî رحمۃ اللہ علیہ wherein he has collected the fabricated narrations on p.38. (There are reservations with regard to the narration of Ibn Mâjah, *'There is no Mahdî except Îsâ.* This we have mentioned separately.)

(6) AHÂDÎTH PERTAINING TO HADRAT MAHDÎ ؑ IN OTHER HADÎTH BOOKS

The following Hadîth scholars have made special mention of Hadrat Mahdî ؑ in their books:

1. Imâm Ahmad رحمۃ اللہ علیہ
2. Imâm Bazzâr رحمۃ اللہ علیہ
3. Ibn Abî Shaybah رحمۃ اللہ علیہ
4. Imâm Hâkim رحمۃ اللہ علیہ
5. Imâm Tabrânî رحمۃ اللہ علیہ
6. Imâm Abû Ya'lâ Mûsilî رحمۃ اللہ علیہ
7. Imâm 'Abdur Razzâq bin Humâm رحمۃ اللہ علیہ

---

[54] The six most authentic compilations of Ahâdîth according to the Hadîth scholars, namely, Sahîh al Bukhârî, Sahîh Muslim, Jâmi' at Tirmidhî, Sunan Abû Dâwûd, Sunan Nasâ'î, Sunan Ibn Mâjah. – [T]

8. Imâm Nuʿaym bin Hammâd – the Shaykh of Imâm Bukhârî رحمه الله
9. Hâfiz Nûr ud Dîn ʿAlî bin Abî Bakr Al Haythamî رحمه الله
10. ʿAllâmah ʿAlâ' ud Dîn ʿAlî al Muttaqî رحمه الله in *Kanz ul ʿUmmâl*

Note: Hâfiz Ibn Taymiyyah رحمه الله in *Minhâj us Sunnah* and Hâfiz Dhahabî رحمه الله in *Mukhtasar Minhâj us Sunnah* have explained,

فنقول : الأحاديث التي تحتج بها على خروج المهدي صحيحة ، رواها أحمد وأبو داؤد والترمذي. ترجمان السنة ص ٣٧٨

The Ahâdîth from which the emergence of Hadrat Mahdî رضي الله عنه have been inferred are authentic. Imâm Ahmad رحمه الله, Imâm Abû Dâwûd رحمه الله and Imâm Tirmidhî رحمه الله have recorded them.[55]

(7). THE APPEARANCE OF MAHDÎ رضي الله عنه IN THE *SAHÎHAYN*[56]

Explanation concerning Hadrat Mahdî رضي الله عنه is found in the *sahîhayn* with clear indication.

Hadîth One:

عن أبي هريرة رضي الله عنه قال : قال رسول الله صلى الله عليه وسلم "كيف أنتم إذا نزل ابن مريم فيكم وإمامكم منكم " . تابعه عقيل والأوزاعي . صحيح البخاري ١/٤٩٠

---

[55] Tarjumân us Sunnah p.378
[56] Sahîh al Bukhârî and Sahîh Muslim

Hadrat Abû Hurayrah ❖ *narrates that Rasûlullâh* ﷺ *said, "What will be your condition when Îsâ bin Maryam will descend among you while your leader will be from among you, (i.e. Hadrat Mahdî* ❖*)."*

a) 'Allâmah Ibn Hajar 'Asqalânî رحمة الله writes in the commentary of *'while your leader will be from among you'*,

وقال أبو الحسن الخسعي الآبدي في مناقب الشافعي : تواترت الأخبار بأن المهدي من هذه الامة وأن عيسى يصلي خلفه ، ذكر ذلك ردا للحديث الذي أخرجه ابن ماجة عن أنس رضي الله عنه ، وفيه "ولا مهدي إلا عيسى" . فتح الباري ٦/٦١١

Abû al Hasan al Khasa'î al Âbidî says in *Manâqib ash Shâfi'î*, 'The Ahâdîth explaining that Mahdî (❖) is from this *ummah* and that 'Îsâ (عليه السلام) will perform *salâh* behind him have reached the level of *tawâtur* (see footnote 50). This explanation has been given in refutation of the Hadîth transmitted by *Ibn Mâjah*, reported by Hadrat Anas ❖, "There is no Mahdî except 'Îsâ."[57]

b) This explanation has also been given by 'Allâmah Badr ud Dîn 'Aynî رحمة الله in *Umdatul Qârî*, commentary of *Sahîh al Bukhârî* vol.16 p.40.

c) There is a *mutâbi*'[58] narration of Hadrat Jâbir bin 'Abdullâh ❖ in *Sahîh Muslim*. The wording is, *'Their leader will say, "Come, lead us in salâh…"*

---

[57] Fath al Bârî vol.6 p.611

[58] If it is understood that a particular narration is the only one regarding a specific subject, but another narrator supports it (in another narration) on condition that

'Allâmah Shabbîr Ahmad 'Uthmânî رحمة الله عليه, commentator of Sahîh *Muslim* says,

أميرهم هو امام المسلمين المهدي الموعود المسعود . فتح الملهم ١/٣٠٣

'Their leader' only refers to the honourable promised leader of the believers, (Hadrat) Mahdî (رضي الله عنه).[59]

d) The above interpretation has been verified by Abû 'Abdullâh Muhammad bin Khalfah Al Washtâtî Al Mâlikî رحمة الله عليه in *Ikmâl u Ikmâl Al Mu'lim,* and by Abû 'Abdullâh Muhammad bin Muhammad bin Yûsuf As Sanûsî Al Hasanî رحمة الله عليه in *Mukammal Ikmâl il Ikmâl.*[60]

e) The following *maqtû'*[61] narration of *Musannaf 'Abdur Razzâq* also corroborates the interpretation of *'Your leader from among you'* to be Hadrat Mahdî رضي الله عنه,

أخبرنا عبد الرزاق ، عن معمر قال : كان ابن سيرين يرى أنـه المهـدي الـذي يصلي وراءه عيسى . مصنف عبد الرزاق ١١/٣٩٩

'Abdur Razzâq has informed us from Ma'mar that he said, "Ibn Sîrîn was of the view that it is Hadrat Mahdî رضي الله عنه who will perform *salâh* behind Hadrat 'Îsâ عليه السلام."[62]

---

the sahâbî in both narrations are the same. The second supporting narration is called *Mutâbi'*. [Irshâd Usûl ul Hadîth p.76] – [T]

[59] Fath al Mulhim vol.1 p.303

[60] vol.1 p.268

[61] A narration whose chain ends at a tâbi'î or tab' ut tâbi'î or a narration that details the statements and actions of the tâbi'în is called *Maqtû'*. [Irshâd Usûl ul Hadîth p.56] – [T]

f) Mullâ ʿAlî al Qârî رحمة الله عليه says,

وإمامكم منكم أى من أهل دينكم ، وقيل من قريش وهو المهدي . مرقاة المفاتيح ١٠/٢٣٢

'From among you' means a common religion, or it is said to mean from the Quraysh and this implies that it is Hadrat Mahdî رضي الله عنه.[63]

g) ʿAllâmah Anwar Shâh Kashmîrî رحمة الله عليه writes in the commentary of this Hadîth,

والمتبادر منه (من لفظ وإمامكم) الإمام المهدي . فيض الباري ٤/٤٥

The apparent comprehended meaning of the words *'Your leader'* is Hadrat Mahdî رضي الله عنه.[64]

He further writes,

وقد اختلط فيه بعض الرواة عند مسلم ، فأطلقه على عيسى عليه الصلوة والسلام فجعل اللفظ "وأمكم منكم" يعني أنه وإن كان من بني اسرائيل لكنه يكون تابعا لشرعكم – والراجح عندي لفظ البخاري أى "وامامكم منكم" بالجملة الأسمية ، والمراد منه الإمام المهدي لما عند ابن ماجة . أيضا ٤/٤٥

Some narrators of Muslim have overlooked certain aspects in this narration. They have taken Hadrat ʿÎsâ عليه السلام to be implied at this juncture. They have narrated the words *'and your leader from among you'*, i.e. even though he is of the Banî Isrâ'îl, he will be a

---

[62] Musannaf ʿAbdur Razzâq vol.11 p.399
[63] Mirqât ul Mafâtîh vol.10 p.232
[64] Fayd al Bârî vol.4 p.45

follower of your *sharî'ah*. According to my understanding, the wording of Sahîh *al Bukhârî* is preferred, i.e. 'and your leader from among you' – as a *jumlah ismiyyah*[65]. The implication in this case will be Hadrat Mahdî ﵁. This implication is corroborated by the narration of *Ibn Mâjah*.[66]

Hadîth Two:

عن أبي سعيد رضي الله عنه قال : قال رسول الله صلى الله عليه وسلم : "من خلفائكم خليفة يحثو المال حثيا ولا يعد عددا" . صحيح مسلم ٢/٣٩٥

Hadrat Abû Sa'îd ﵁ narrates that Rasûlullâh ﷺ said, "There will be a khalîfah from among your khulafâ' who will distribute wealth unstintingly."[67]

Hadîth Three:

عن أبي سعيد وجابر رضي الله عنهما قال : قال رسول الله صلى الله عليه وسلم "يكون في آخر الزمان خليفة يقسم المال ولا يعده" . أيضا

Hadrat Abû Sa'îd ﵁ and Hadrat Jâbir ﵁ narrate that Rasûlullâh ﷺ said, "There will be a khalîfah during the final era who will distribute wealth unstintingly."[68]

---

[65] A sentence beginning with a noun – [T]
[66] Ibid
[67] Sahîh Muslim vol.2 p.395
[68] Ibid

Maulânâ Badr e ʿÂlam Mîrthî ﵀ writes,

It should remain clear that it is proven from the Ahâdîth of *Sahîh Muslim* that there will be a *khalîfah* of the Muslims in the final era. In his time, great blessings will descend. He will be born before Hadrat ʿÎsâ ﵊. Dajjâl will emerge in his time and he (Dajjâl) will be killed at the hands of Hadrat ʿÎsâ ﵊. This *khalîfah* would have taken the place as the *imâm* of *salâh* when Hadrat ʿÎsâ ﵊ will descend from the skies. He will step back upon seeing Hadrat ʿÎsâ ﵊. Hadrat ʿÎsâ ﵊ will say to him, "You have the right of leading the *salâh* (*imâmah*) because you have already taken the place as *imâm*. This is a honour for this *ummah*." Hadrat ʿÎsâ ﵊ will perform this *salâh* following Hadrat Mahdî ﵁.

All these qualities are proven in authentic Ahâdîth that the scholars of Hadîth have not criticized. The only thing that remains to be discussed is whether this *khalîfah* is Hadrat Mahdî ﵁ or another *khalîfah*. Other Ahâdîth clearly state that this *khalîfah* is Hadrat Mahdî ﵁.

According to us, once this *khalîfah* has been mentioned in *Sahîh Muslim*, and the other Hadîth books clearly state this *khalîfah's* name with the same details as in *Sahîh Muslim*, then, these other Ahâdîth should be understood to be in the same category as those of *Sahîh Muslim*. Therefore, there is scope to state that the emergence of Hadrat Mahdî ﵁ is proven from *Sahîh Muslim* directly.

An example of this is that when a Hadîth of *Sahîh Muslim* states that when Hadrat ʿÎsâ ﵊ will descend, then one leader of the Muslims would have taken the place in front to lead the *salâh*. There are other Ahâdîth that explain the name of this leader as Hadrat Mahdî ﵁. Certainly, these Ahâdîth will stand as the explanation of the unclear Hadîth. Another example; a Hadîth of

Sahîh Muslim states that there will be a *khalîfah* towards the end of time who will distribute wealth generously. It is proven from other Ahâdîth that generosity of this nature will be found in the era of Hadrat Mahdî. Therefore, it is correct to state that the Ahâdîth of *Sahîh Muslim* refer to Hadrat Mahdî.

Similarly, with regards to the Ahâdîth about wars that are narrated in *Sahîh Muslim*, if it is explained in other Ahâdîth that these same incidents are to happen in the era of Hadrat Mahdî, then it stands to reason that the narrations of *Sahîh Muslim* refer to the incidents of the era of Hadrat Mahdî. In all probability, the scholars of Hadîth have understood some unclear Ahâdîth to refer to Hadrat Mahdî upon this basis, and have recorded them in the chapters pertaining to Hadrat Mahdî. Like Imâm Abû Dawûd indicates towards the twelfth Imâm to be Hadrat Mahdî by recording the Hadîth of the twelve Imâms in the chapter of Hadrat Mahdî.[69]

Hadîth Four:

عن جابر بن عبد الله رضي الله عنه ، سمعت النبي صلى الله عليه وسلم يقول :

"لا تزال طائفة من أمتي يقاتلون على الحق ظاهرين إلى يوم القيامة ، قال :

فينزل عيسى بن مريم صلى الله عليه وسلم فيقول أميرهم : تعال صل لنا ،

فيقول : لا ، إن بعضكم على بعض أمراء ، تكرمة الله هذه الأمة . صحيح

مسلم ١/٨٧

---

[69] Tarjumân us Sunnah vol.4 pp.378, 379

H̲ad̲rat Jâbir bin 'Abdullâh ﷺ narrates that he heard Rasûlullâh ﷺ saying, "There will be a group in my ummah that will remain firm upon the truth until Qiyâmah. Then when Îsâ bin Maryam will descend, their leader will say, "Come, lead us in s̲alâh." He will reply, "No. Some of you are leaders over others. This is a bounty of Allâh upon this ummah."

The leader of the Muslims in the above H̲adîth refers to H̲ad̲rat Mahdî ﷺ. 'Allâmah Shabbîr Ah̲mad 'Uthmânî رحمة الله عليه explains this in *Fath̲ al Mulhim,*

قوله "فيقول اميرهم الخ" هو امام المسلمين المهدي الموعود المسعود . فتح الملهم ١/٣٠٣

The Imâm of the Muslims, the promised, fortunate *Mahdî* is meant by *'Their leader will say'.*[70]

We come to know from this text of 'Allâmah Shabbîr Ah̲mad 'Uthmânî رحمة الله عليه that all the Ah̲âdîth on this subject that vaguely state the word *'leader'* or *'khalîfah'* refer to H̲ad̲rat Mahdî ﷺ.[71] We will also mention a narration of *S̲ah̲îh̲ Muslim*[72] about the *Mahdî* in the forthcoming pages.

Note: A number of authors in the past, as well as a few today reject the belief of the emergence of *Mahdî* simply upon the basis that H̲ad̲rat Mahdî ﷺ is not mentioned in the *s̲ah̲îh̲ayn*. We hope that this explanation removes any misgivings in this regard. Allâh ﷻ states,

---

[70] Fath̲ al Mulhim vol.1 p.303

[71] 'Aqîdah Z̲uhûr e Mahdî p.62

[72] vol.2 p.388, H̲adîth 2884

فَمَن جَاءَهُ مَوْعِظَةٌ مِّن رَّبِّهِ فَانتَهَى فَلَهُ مَا سَلَفَ

The one to whom the advice from his Rabb had come and he refrained, then for him is that which has passed. [Sûrah al Baqarah (the Bull) 2:275]

HADRAT ʿÎSÂ عليه السلام AND HADRAT MAHDÎ رضي الله عنه ARE TWO DIFFERENT PEOPLE

حدثنا يونس بن عبد الأعلى ، حدثنا محمد بن ادريس الشافعي ، حدثني محمد بن خالد الجندي ، عن أبان بن صالح ، عن الحسن ، عن أنس بن مالك أن رسول الله صلى الله عليه وسلم قال : "لا يزداد الأمر الا شدة ، ولا الدنيا الا ادبارا ، ولا الناس الا شحا ، ولا تقوم الساعة الا على شرار الناس ، ولا المهدي الا عيسى بن مريم " . ابن ماجة ٣٠٢ والمسند الجامع رقم ١٦٠٠

Hadrat Anas bin Mâlik رضي الله عنه narrates that Rasûlullâh ﷺ said, "The matter will increase in severity, the world will retrogress, people will become stingy, Qiyâmah will not happen except upon the worst of people and there is no Mahdî except ʿÎsâ."[73]

It is apparently proven from this Hadîth that the promised *Mahdî* is none other than Hadrat ʿÎsâ عليه السلام. There is none else to emerge as the *Mahdî*. Two answers to this are provided here.

1. The grading of this Hadîth is debated. *(mutakallam fîh)*
2. The interpretation of this Hadîth is demanded rather than the apparent wording.

---

[73] Sunan Ibn Mâjah p.302, Al Musnad Al Jâmiʿ Hadîth 1600

1. The grading of this Hadîth is debated. *(mutakallam fîh)*
Hâfiz Dhahabî رحمه الله in *Mîzân al I'tidâl* states the following under the biography of Muhammad bin Khâlid al Janadî,

قلت : حديثه لا مهدي إلا عيسى بن مريم ، وهو خبر منكر . ٣/٥٢

The Hadîth *'There is no Mahdî except Îsâ'* narrated by him is *munkar.*[74]

One of the reasons why this narration is *munkar*[75] is that it is based on the narrator, Muhammad bin Khâlid al Janadî who is alone in narrating this, and he is highly debated about *(mutakallam fih)*. Hâfiz Dhahabî رحمه الله writes about him,

قال الأزدي : منكر الحديث ، وقال عبد الله الحاكم : مجهول . أيضا

Azdî says, 'he is *munkar al hadîth*[76], and 'Abdullâh al Hâkim says, *'he is majhûl*[77]'. Hâfiz Ibn Hajar 'Asqalânî رحمه الله writes concerning Muhammad bin Khalid al Janadî,

"قال الآبري : محمد بن خالد غير معروف عند أهل الصناعة من أهل النقل"

Al Âbirî said, "Muhammad bin Khalid is *ghayr ma'rûf*[78] according to the scholars of narration."

---

[74] Mîzân al I'tidâl vol.3 p.52

[75] *Munkar* is a narration whose narrator makes a lot of mistakes or is very negligent and forgetful or he is responsible for any other open sin besides lying and innovation. [Irshâd Usûl ul Hadîth p.116] – [T]

[76] *Munkar al Hadîth* refers to a narrator that has narrated many *Munkar* narrations. He deserves to be left aside. [Irshâd Usûl ul Hadîth p.117] – [T]

[77] *Majhûl* refers to something that is unknown. It refers to a narration whose narrator is not known because his name was not mentioned in the chain. [Irshâd Usûl ul Hadîth pp.101-102] – [T]

[78] Unknown – [T]

He further explains,

"وقال البيهقي : قال أبو عبد الله الحافظ : محمد بن خالد مجهـول " . تهـذيب التهذيب ٩/١٤٤

Bayhaqî said, Hâfiz Abû ʿAbdullâh said, "Muhammad bin Khalid is *majhûl*."[79]

Hâfiz Jalâl ud Dîn Suyutî رحمة الله عليه has written at length on this Hadîth in his *Misbâh az Zujâjah,* marginal notes of *Sunan Ibn Mâjah*. We feel it appropriate to present a summary of it here, ʿAllâmah رحمة الله عليه has scrutinized the rejection and acceptance of this narration by the scholars as well as the criticism of the debated narrators[80] with his special sight into research and his in depth study. Abul Hasan ʿAlî bin Muhammad bin ʿAbdullâh al Wâsitî رحمة الله عليه has mentioned a dream in this regard, in which he saw Imâm Shâfiʿî رحمة الله عليه. Imâm Shâfiʿî رحمة الله عليه said to him that Yûnus bin ʿAbdul Aʿlâ has wrongly attributed this narration to me. He has also mentioned the answer that Ibn Kathîr رحمة الله عليه has explained.[81]

The author of Nibrâs says,

لأن الحديث لا يصح . نبراس ٣١٥

This hadîth is not authentic.[82]

---

79 Tahdhîb ut Tahdhîb vol.9 p.144

80 Yûnus bin ʿAbdul Aʿlâ رحمة الله عليه and Muhammad bin Khalid al Janadî رحمة الله عليه

81 Misbâh az Zujâjah, marginal notes of Sunan Ibn Mâjah p.300

82 Nibrâs p.315

A text of *Minhâj us Sunnah* states,

فأما حديث لا مهـدي إلا عيـسى بـن مـريم فـضعيف ، فـلا يعـارض هـذه

الأحاديث . منهاج السنة ٥٦٢

The Hadîth 'There is no *Mahdî* except 'Îsâ' is *da'îf*.[83] For this reason, it cannot be contrasted with this one.[84]

'Allâmah Saghânî رحمه الله has classified this narration to be *maudû'*.[85]

2. The interpretation of this Hadîth is demanded rather than the apparent wording.

The author of *Misbâh az Zujâjah* has written in the marginal notes of this Hadîth,

وهذا الحديث فيما يظهر ببادي الـرأي مخـالف للأحاديـث الـواردة في إثبـات

مهدي غير عيسى بن مريم ، وعند التأمل لا ينافيها ، بل يكون المراد من ذلك

أن المهدي حق الهدى هو عيسى بن مريم عليـه الـسلام ، ولا ينـافي ذلـك أن

يكون غيره مهديا أيضا . مصباح الزجاجة ٣٠

[83] *Da'îf* is translated as weak. It refers to such a Hadîth in which the conditions of *Sahîh* and *Hasan* are not found. [Irshâd Usûl ul Hadîth p.121] – [T]

[84] Minhâj us Sunnah p.562

[85] Al Fawâid Al Majmû'a bi al Ahâdîth ad Da'îfah p.195 (Chapter of Miscellaneous narrations, Hadîth 127, Tadhkiratul Maudû'ât p.223 (Chapter on the Final Age and its trials) A *Maudû'* narration is one from whose narrator lies have been proven, even if one lie was spoken by him, all his narrations will not be accepted. The narrations of such a narrator are not accepted according to the Hadîth scholars. [Irshâd Usûl ul Hadîth p.99] – [T]

Outwardly, it seems that this Ḥadîth contradicts those that explain of a Mahdî besides ʿÎsâ (عليه السلام). However, upon careful scrutiny and thought, we understand that there is no contradiction between the two, considering the purport of the two. The meaning of the above narration is that the title 'Mahdî' refers to Ḥadrat ʿÎsâ عليه السلام to a complete degree. And Ḥadrat ʿÎsâ عليه السلام being a Mahdî does not negate another person being a Mahdî.[86]

We learn that this narration cannot be used as proof. The subject matter of this narration also deserves scrutiny in the light of a comprehensive study of the subject. The reason for this is that there are a number of Aḥâdîth before us that clearly state that Ḥadrat ʿÎsâ عليه السلام and Ḥadrat Mahdî رضى الله عنه are two different people. These narrations are presented below,

لن تهلك امة أنا في أولها وعيسى بن مريم في آخرها والمهدي في أوسطها . أبــو نعيم في أخبار المهدي عن ابن عباس . كنز العمال ١٤/٢٦٦ رقم ٣٨٦٧١

That ummah will never be destroyed, at whose beginning I am, at whose ending will be Îsâ bin Maryam and whose middle period will have Mahdî among them.[87]

منا الذي يصلي عيسى بن مريم خلفه . أبو نعيم في أخبار المهدي عن أبي سعيد . كنز العمال ١٤/٢٦٦ رقم ٣٨٦٧٣

The person behind whom Îsâ bin Maryam will perform ṣalâh is from among us.[88]

---

[86] See Misbâh az Zujâjah for a detailed commentary
[87] Kanz ul ʿUmmâl vol.14 p.266, Ḥadîth 38671
[88] Kanz ul ʿUmmâl vol.14 p.266, Ḥadîth 38673

عن عبد الله بن عمر رضي الله عنه قال : "المهدي الذي ينزل عليه عيسى بن مريم ويصلي خلفه عيسى" . أخرجه نعيم بن حماد ٢٦٤ رقم ١٠٤٢ كذا في الحاوي ٢/٧٨

It is narrated from Hadrat 'Abdullâh bin 'Umar ﷺ that he said, "Mahdî will emerge after Îsâ and Îsâ will perform (one) salâh behind him."

"لا تزال طائفة من امتي تقاتل عن الحق حتى ينزل عيسى بن مريم عند طلوع الفجر ببيت المقدس ، ينزل على المهدي فيقال له تقدم يا نبي الله فصل لنا ، فيقول : ان هذه الامة أمين بعضهم على بعض لكرامتهم على الله عز وجل" . أخرجه أبو عمرو الداني في سننه عن جابر بن عبد الله رضي الله عنه ٢٤٠ رقم ٦٨٦ والحاوي ٢/٨٣

There will always be a group among my ummah who will fight in defence of the truth until Îsâ bin Maryam descends upon Bayt al Muqaddas[89] at the time of Fajr. It will be requested of him, "O messenger of Allâh, lead us in salâh." He will say, "In this ummah, some lead others." [Similar wording is found in Sahîh Muslim]

"يلتفت المهدي وقد نزل عيسى بن مريم كأنما يقطر من شعره الماء ، فيقول المهدي : تقدم صل بالناس ، فيقول عيسى : إنما أقيمت الصلوة لك ، فيصلي

---

89 In Jerusalem

خلف رجل من ولدي" . أخرجه أبو عمرو الداني في سننه عن حذيفة رضي
الله عنه في سياق حديث طويل في باب ما روي في الوقيعة اللتي تكون
بالزوراء الخ ص ٢٠٢ إلى ٢٠٩   رقم ٥٩٦

*Mahdî would turn to ʿÎsâ bin Maryam when the latter would have
descended (from the sky). (His hair will be in such a condition) that it
would be as if water is dripping from it. Mahdî will say, "Come
forward, lead us in ṣalâh." ʿÎsâ will reply, "The iqâmah has been
called out for you." He (ʿÎsâ) will perform ṣalâh led by a person from
my progeny."[90]*

عن جابر رضي الله عنه قال : قال رسول الله صلى الله عليه وسلم : ينزل
عيسى بن مريم فيقول أميرهم المهدي : تعال صل بنا ، فيقول : وان بعضكم
على بعض أمراء ، تكرمة الله لهذه الأمة . أخرجه السيوطي في الحاوي ٦٤/٢
عن أبي نعيم

*It is narrated from Ḥaḍrat Jâbir ☼ that he said, "Rasulullâh ﷺ said,
"ʿÎsâ bin Maryam will descend, then their leader Mahdî will say to
him, 'Come, lead us in ṣalâh.' He will reply, 'Some of you are leaders
over the others. This is the honour of Allâh upon this ummah.'"[91]*

---

[90] Sunan of Abû ʿAmr Dânî pp.202-209, Ḥadîth 596
[91] Al Ḥâwî vol.2 p.64 from Abû Nuʿaym

عن ابن سيرين رحمه الله قال : المهدي من هذه الأمة ، وهو الذي يؤم عيسى بن مريم عليهما السلام . أخرجه ابن أبي شيبة ١٥/١٩٨ رقم ١٩٤٩٥ كذا في الحاوي ٢/٦٥

It is narrated from Ibn Sîrîn رحمه الله that he said, "The Mahdî is an individual of this ummah. It is he who will lead Îsâ bin Maryam عليه السلام in salâh."[92]

عن أبي أمامة رضي الله عنه قال : خطبنا رسول الله صلى الله عليه وسلم وذكر الدجال ، وقال : "فتنفى المدينة الخبث منها كما ينفي الكير خبث الحديد ، ويدعى ذلك اليوم يوم الخلاص ، فقالت ام شريك : فأين العرب يا رسول الله يومئذ ؟ قال : هم يومئذ قليل ، وجلهم بيت المقدس ، وامامهم المهدي رجل صالح ، فبينما امامهم قد تقدم يصلي بهم الصبح اذ نزل عليهم عيسى بن مريم الصبح ، فرجع ذلك الامام ينكص يمشي القهقرى ليتقدم عيسى ، فيضع عيسى يده بين كتفيه ، ثم يقول له تقدم : فانها لك اقيمت ، فيصلي بهم امامهم " . أخرجه ابن ماجة رقم ٤٠٧٧ والروياني وابن خريمة وأبو عوانة والحاكم وأبو نعيم – واللفظ له – كذا في الحاوي ٢/٦٥

It is narrated from Hadrat Abû Umâmah رضي الله عنه that he said, "Rasûlullâh ﷺ delivered a sermon in which he discussed Dajjâl. He said, "Madînah will remove its dirt just as a furnace removes dirt from steel. That day will be called 'The Day of Release'. Umm e Sharîk

---

92 Musannaf Ibn Abî Shaybah vol.15 p.198, Narration 19495, Al Hâwî vol.2 p.65

enquired, "O Messenger of Allâh, where will the Arabs be on that day?" Rasûlullâh ﷺ replied, "They will be very few and will be located in Bayt al Muqaddas. Their leader 'Mahdî' will be a pious person. Their Imâm would have come forward to lead them in Fajr ṣalâh when Îsâ bin Maryam will descend among them. This Imâm will walk back on his heels in acceptance so that Îsâ may come forward. Îsâ will place his hands between his (Mahdî's) shoulders and say to him, "Go forward, because the iqâmah was called out for you." Then their leader (Mahdî ﷺ) will lead them in ṣalâh."[93]

Summary:

In the light of all these narrations it is known with definite certainty that Haḍrat Mahdî ﷺ and Haḍrat 'Îsâ عليه السلام are two different people. Also, in various places in the Saḥîḥayn it is explained that the descent of Haḍrat 'Îsâ عليه السلام will take place at such a time when the Muslims will have a leader amongst them. There is not a single ḍa 'îf (see footnote 83) narration that states that Haḍrat Mahdî ﷺ is not meant by the narrations that clearly state his name. Consequently, it has become clear that Haḍrat 'Îsâ عليه السلام and Haḍrat Mahdî ﷺ are two different people, and not one person with two names.

Despite this, if the narration of Sunan Ibn Mâjah 'There is no Mahdî except 'Îsâ' is accepted to a certain degree, then its explanation is as stated below:

1. The meaning of referring to Haḍrat 'Îsâ عليه السلام as Mahdî is 'A 'dham al Mahdî' (the Greatest Mahdî). This is because every guided person and every person who guides others can be called 'Mahdî' in the light of its lexical implication. Imâm Suyûṭî عليه الرحمة has

---

[93] Al Ḥâwî vol.2 p.65

recorded the following statement of Ḥaḍrat ʿAbdullâh bin ʿUmar

عن ابن عمر رضي الله عنه قال لابن الحنفية : المهدي الذي يقولون كما يقول :
الرجل الصالح ، اذا كان الرجل صالحا قيل لـه المهـدي . الحـاوي للفتاوى
٢/٧٨ وكذا معناه في الفتن لنعيم بن حماد ٢٦٣ رقم ١٠٣٧

The *Mahdî*, as is commonly used, is like a person saying, 'A pious person. This is because if a person is pious, he is called *Mahdî*'. (In the light of this, '*Mahdî*' can refer to a number of people in its general implication).[94]

It is quite apparent that in consideration of this lexical meaning, there will be many individuals found from after Rasûlullâh ﷺ until today that could be called '*Mahdî*'. Rasûlullâh ﷺ himself used the word '*Mahdiyyîn*' for the *khulafâ' e râshidîn*. Ḥaḍrat ʿÎsâ ﷺ is referred to as the highest ranking rightful *Mahdî*. Ibn al Qayyim ﷺ points to this in the following words,

"لأن عيسى أعظم مهدي بين يـدي رسـول الله صلـى الله عليـه وسلم وبـين
الساعة ...إلى أن قال : فيصح أن يقال : لا مهدي في الحقيقة سواه ، وان كـان
غيره مهديا" . المنار المنيف ١٤٨

'Îsâ is the greatest *Mahdî* after the era of Rasûlullâh ﷺ until Qiyâmah...it is correct to state, 'There is no genuine *Mahdî* except him even though others can be (called) *Mahdî*.

Similarly, it is said, '*Ḥajj is ʿArafah*'. The meaning of this is not that only *wuqûf* in *ʿarafah* constitutes Ḥajj. However, it means that it is an important link in the chain of Ḥajj. In the same way,

---

94 Al Ḥâwî vol.2 p.78

the word *'Dajjâl'* can refer to many people who possess the qualities of *Dajjâl* when considering the lexical meaning of the word *'Dajjâl'*. The real and complete reference of the word, however, is to the great liar, *Dajjâl,* who will emerge in the time of Hadrat Mahdî ﷺ and Hadrat 'Îsâ عليه السلام.

2. Another interpretation could be that a *Mahdî* who is complete and sinless is Hadrat 'Îsâ عليه السلام. Ibn al Qayyim رحمه الله writes,

وكما يصح أن يقال : إنما المهدي عيسى بن مريم ، يعني المهدي الكامل المعصوم . كذا قال القرطبي في التذكرة ٧٠١ وفي الحاوي عن القرطبي ٢/٨٦

It is correct to say, 'The only *Mahdî* is 'Îsâ bin Maryam, i.e. the complete and sinless *Mahdî.'*

Shaykh Barzanjî رحمه الله also writes along similar lines,

لا مهدي معصوما مطلقا إلا عيسى عليه السلام . الاشاعة ١٤٣

There is no sinless general *Mahdî* except 'Îsâ عليه السلام.[95]

3. The above interpretation is clarified by the following *Athar* (see footnote 2) of Walîd bin Muslim رحمه الله, as recorded by 'Allâmah Suyûtî رحمه الله.

عن الوليد بن مسلم رحمه الله قال : سمعت رجلا يحدث قوما ، فقال : المهديون ثلاثة ، مهدي الخير عمر بن عبد العزيز رحمه الله ، ومهدي الدم وهو الذي تسكن عليه الدماء ومهدي الدين عيسى بن مريم – تسلم أمته في زمانه

---

[95] Al Ishâ'a p.143

. وأخرج أيضا عن كعب رضي الله عنه قال : مهـدي الخير (المهـدي المنتظر محمد بن عبد الله) يخرج بعد السفياني . العرف الوردي في أخبار المهـدي ٣٥ الحاوي ٢/٧٨ الفتن لنعيم بن حماد ٢٥٣ رقم ٩٨٨

It is narrated from Walîd bin Muslim رحمة الله عليه that he said, "I heard a person who was delivering a lesson of Hadîth saying, 'There are three *Mahdî's,* one is the *Mahdî* of goodness, 'Umar bin 'Abdul 'Azîz رحمة الله عليه, the second is the *Mahdî* of blood, upon whose hands bloodshed will come to an end and the third is the *Mahdî* of *dîn,* 'Îsâ bin Maryam, upon whom the entire *ummah* in his time will bring faith. There is another narration from Hadrat Ka'b رضي الله عنه that explains that the *Mahdî* of goodness (the awaited *Mahdî,* Muhammad bin 'Abdullâh) will emerge after *Sufyânî.*[96]

4. One interpretation is that there is an implicit text here. The complete text would read as follows,

لا قول للمهدي الا بمشورة عيسى عليه السلام . الاشاعة ١٤٣

Mahdî will consult with 'Îsâ عليه السلام in all affairs.[97]

The above answers can be presented as the interpretation of all those Ahâdîth whose subject matter could cause one to fall into error, thinking Hadrat 'Îsâ عليه السلام and Hadrat Mahdî رضي الله عنه to be the same person. A narration of *Musnad Bazzâr,* narrated by Hadrat Abû Hurayrah رضي الله عنه, shows this,

---

[96] Al 'Urf al Wardî fî Akhbâr al Mahdî p.35, Al Hâwî vol.2 p.78, Al Fitan p.253, Narration 988

[97] Al Îshâ'a p.143

عن أبي هريرة رضي الله عنه قال : قال رسول الله صلى الله عليه وسلم : يوشك من عاش منكم أن يخرج المهدي عيسى بن مريم اماما مهديا وحكما عدلا الخ . عارضة الأحوذي ٩/٧٧

Rasûlullâh ﷺ said, "Those of you who will live will see Mahdî, i.e. Îsâ bin Maryam. He will emerge as guided, an Imâm and a just ruler.[98]

The summary of this discussion is that Hadrat ʻÎsâ عليه السلام and Hadrat Mahdî رضي الله عنه are two different people. Therefore, those who have moved away from the path of truth, believing Hadrat ʻÎsâ عليه السلام and Hadrat Mahdî رضي الله عنه to be one and the same person are in reality denying Hadrat Mahdî رضي الله عنه. Such a person is astray. This is especially true with regards to the *Qâdiyânî* sect who first believed Hadrat ʻÎsâ عليه السلام and Hadrat Mahdî رضي الله عنه to be one and the same person. Thereafter they said that this person is Mirzâ Ghulâm Ahmad Qâdiyânî (upon him be what he deserves). They are certainly very far from the path of truth and are wandering in the valley of deviation. In fact, the following verse illustrates their reality,

ظُلُمَاتٌ بَعْضُهَا فَوْقَ بَعْضٍ إِذَا أَخْرَجَ يَدَهُ لَمْ يَكَدْ يَرَاهَا

Darkness upon darkness. (The darkness is so intense that) He is unable to see his own hand when he extends it before himself. [Surah an Nûr (Celestial Light) 24:40]

The truth is that none of the signs regarding the awaited *Mahdî,* Muhammad bin ʻAbdullâh رضي الله عنه and Hadrat ʻÎsâ عليه السلام are found in Mirzâ Ghulâm Ahmad Qâdiyânî to the least extent.

---

[98] Musnad Bazzâr vol.9 p.77

THE BELIEF OF THE EMERGENCE OF *MAHDÎ*

1. It is necessary and obligatory for every Muslim to believe in the emergence of *Mahdî*.

وبالجملة فالتصديق بخروجه (اى المهدي) واجب . نبراس ٣٠٥

In summary, it is obligatory to verify, i.e. believe in the emergence of *Mahdî*.[99]

The following is explained in *Sharh ʿAqîdah as Safârînî*,

فالإيمان بخروج المهدي واجب ، كما هو مقرر عند أهل العلم ، ومدون في عقائد أهل السنة والجماعة. شرح عقيدة السفاريني ٢/٨٠

It is obligatory to have belief in the emergence of *Mahdî*. This is established according to the scholars and is recorded in the books of the *Ahl us Sunnah wal Jamâʿah*.

ʿAllâmah Muhammad bin Sulaymân al Halabî رحمة الله عليه writes,

واعلم أنه يجب الإيمان بنزول عيسى عليه السلام وكذا بخروج المهدي .

نخبة اللآلي لشرح بدء الأمالي ٧١

Know well that it is obligatory to believe in the descent of ʿÎsâ عليه السلام. Similarly, (it is obligatory to believe in the) emergence of *Mahdî*.[100]

Hadrat Shâh Walîullâh Muhaddith Dehlawî رحمة الله عليه says,

The emergence of *Mahdî* close to *Qiyâmah* is a certainty. Hadrat Mahdî رضي الله عنه will be a truthful ruler in the sight of Allâh تعالى and Rasûlullâh ﷺ. Rasûlullâh ﷺ also prophesized him to be a *khalîfah*.

---

99 Nibrâs p.305

100 Nukhbah al La'âlî p.71

He further writes,

It will be obligatory to follow Hadrat Mahdî ﷺ in those matters that deal with the *khalîfah* during his (Hadrat Mahdî ﷺ's) *khilâfah.*[101]

2. The belief of the emergence of *Mahdî* is an accepted belief of the *Ahl us Sunnah wal Jamâ ʿah.*

Maulânâ Badr e ʿÂlam Mîrthî رحمة الله عليه explains in *Tarjumân us Sunnah* that the commentator of *ʿAqîdah As Safârînî* has claimed the emergence of Hadrat Mahdî ﷺ to have reached the level of *tawâtur* (see footnote 50). He has counted it among the beliefs of the *Ahl us Sunnah wal Jamâ ʿah.* He says,

'The Ahâdîth concerning the emergence of Hadrat Mahdî ﷺ are so many that they can be said to have reached the level of *tawâtur ma ʿnawî* (see footnote 51). This aspect is so famous that among them that it is counted to be from the beliefs of the *Ahl us Sunnah.* Abû Nuʿaym رحمة الله عليه, Abû Dâwûd رحمة الله عليه, Tirmidhî رحمة الله عليه, Nasâ'î رحمة الله عليه and others have recorded a number of narrations from the sahâbah ﷺ and the tâbiʿîn on this subject. From these narrations, one attains definite conviction in the emergence of Hadrat Mahdî ﷺ. Therefore, it is necessary to have conviction in the emergence of Hadrat Mahdî ﷺ in accordance to the explanation of the *ʿulemâ'* and the beliefs of the *Ahl us Sunnah wal Jamâ ʿah.*'[102]

3. One attains complete conviction in the emergence of Hadrat Mahdî ﷺ due to the Ahâdîth narrated in this regard.

---

[101] Izâlatul Khifâ' vol.1 p.26

[102] Tarjumân us Sunnah p.377 from Sharh ʿAqîdah As Safârînî

4. Muftî Nizâm ud Dîn Shâmzî رحمة الله عليه says,
'Those who are affiliated with the field of Hadîth are aware of the fact that the scholars of Hadîth record the chapters in their books of those things which, according to them are proven in the Ahâdîth. This is especially the case when after transmitting the Hadîth they remain silent. In accordance to this principle, it can be safely said that those scholars of Hadîth that transmitted Ahâdîth about the emergence of *Mahdî*[103] and recorded separate chapters for these Ahâdîth had the belief of the emergence of Hadrat Mahdî رضي الله عنه. They also had the belief that he (Hadrat Mahdî رضي الله عنه) is one of the signs of *Qiyâmah*.'[104]

5. In every era, from the honourable era of Rasûlullâh ﷺ until today, the *mufassirîn*[105], *mutakallimîn*[106] and most of the *'ulemâ'* of the *ummah* have explained the emergence of *Mahdî* with due importance in their books and statements. 'Abdur Rahmân Mubârakpûrî رحمة الله عليه writes regarding this,

اعلم أن المشهور بين الكافة من أهل الاسلام على ممر الأعصار أنه لا بد في آخر الزمان من ظهور رجل من أهل البيت ... إلى أن قال : ويسمى بالمهدي . تحفة الأحوذي ٦/٤٠١

It should be known that it has remained famous among all the Muslims that in the final era, a person from the *ahl al bayt*[107] will emerge ... his name will be *Mahdî*.[108]

---

[103] This has been explained in the chapter 'Ahâdîth pertaining to the emergence of Hadrat Mahdî رضي الله عنه'

[104] 'Aqîdah Zuhûr e Mahdî

[105] Scholars of *Tafsîr* (Exegesis) – [T]

[106] Scholars of Belief – [T]

[107] The household of Rasûlullâh ﷺ - [T]

[108] Tuhfa al Ahwadhî vol.6 p.401

The conclusion reached is that the vast majority of the Muslim *ummah* believes and accepts the emergence of *Mahdî* with *tawâtur* (see footnote 50).

6. The *ʿulemâ'* of *ʿaqâ'id* have stated the emergence of *Mahdî* to be the truth. Hadrat Muftî Kifâyatullâh رحمة الله عليه says,
'Before *Qiyâmah,* the occurrence of the emergence of *Dajjâl,* the coming of Hadrat Masîh عليه السلام and the emergence of Hadrat Mahdî رضي الله عنه and all those things that are proven from authentic narrations and are worthy of standing as proof are true.'[109]

Hadrat Maulânâ Muhammad Idrîs Kândehlawî رحمة الله عليه writes in *ʿAqâ'id e Islâm,*
'It is among the beliefs of the *ahl us sunnah wal jamâʿah* that the emergence of Hadrat Mahdî رضي الله عنه in the final era is true and accurate. It is necessary to believe in it because the emergence of Hadrat Mahdî رضي الله عنه is proven from *mutawâtir* (see footnote 50) Ahâdîth and by the consensus of the *ummah,* even though some of the details are proven from Ahâdîth classified as *khabar e wâhid*[110]. From the era of the sahâbah رضي الله عنهم and the tâbiʿîn until today, Muslims of every class, in the east and west, the *ʿulemâ',* pious, commoners and elite have been explaining the emergence of Hadrat Mahdî رضي الله عنه.'[111]

---

[109] Jawâhir al Îmân p.8

[110] *Khabar e Wâhid* is literally translated as 'that which has been narrated by a single person'. In the study of Hadîth it refers to such a narration which has not reached the level of *tawâtur.* – [T]

[111] ʿAqâ'id e Islâm vol.1 p.64

THE RULING PERTAINING TO THE PERSON WHO REJECTS THE EMERGENCE OF *MAHDÎ*

The emergence of Hadrat Mahdî ؏ is the unanimous belief of all among the *ahl us sunnah*. Therefore, it cannot be rejected. Faqîh al Ummah Hadrat Muftî Mahmûd al Hasan Gangohî ﵫ writes regarding the rejecter of this belief,

Question:
Is the belief of the emergence of Hadrat Mahdî ؏ among the necessary aspects of *dîn* in the light of the Qur'ân and Hadîth? What is the ruling of *sharî'ah* regarding the person who does not believe in the emergence of Hadrat Mahdî ؏?

Answer:
All praise is due to Allâh, and may His blessings and salutations be upon Rasûlullâh ﷺ

Detail regarding the vicegerent of Allâh - the *Mahdî* - is found in *Sunan Abû Dâwûd*. Mention is made of his signs, the pledge of allegiance at his hands and his works. The person who does not accept his emergence does not accept these Ahâdîth. He should be reformed so that he can tread the straight path.[112]

Hadrat Maulânâ Abû Muhammad 'Abdul Haq Haqqânî ﵫ writes,

'It is part of the beliefs of the *Ahl us Sunnah* that Hadrat Mahdî ؏ will emerge in the final age wherein he will overpower the non Muslims and strengthen Islâm. The rest of the details have been proven from narrations classified as *khabar e âhâd*[113]. These

---

[112] Fatâwâ Mahmûdiyya vol.1 p.111
[113] Plural of *Khabar e Wâhid* – [T]

details are also portions of various a<u>h</u>âdîth that have been strung together. If a person does not have conviction in it, he does not leave the fold of Islâm. It is a separate matter altogether if we err in understanding the narrations passed down to us in whatever way from Rasûlullâh ﷺ. However, all of them are true and will definitely happen. This should be borne in mind with the other signs of *Qiyâmah* as well.[114]

THE CONCERN OF THE <u>SAH</u>ÂBAH ؓ AND STRANGE GLAD-TIDINGS FROM RASÛLULLÂH ﷺ

عن أبي سعيد الخدري رضي الله عنه قال : خشينا أن يكون بعد نبينا حدث ، فسئلنا نبينا صلى الله عليه وسلم فقال : "إن في أمتي المهدي يخرج يعيش خمسا أو سبعا أو تسعا . (زيد الشاك) قال : قلنا : وما ذاك قال : سنين ، قال فيجيء إليه الرجل فيقول : يا مهدي أعطني أعطني قال : فيحثى له في ثوبه ما استطاع أن يحمله" هذا حديث صحيح . ترمذي ٢/٤٧

<u>H</u>a<u>d</u>rat Abû Sa'îd Khu<u>d</u>rî ؓ narrates that Rasûlullâh ﷺ said, "We fear that events would take place after Rasûlullâh ﷺ. We asked Rasûlullâh ﷺ about this. He ﷺ said, "Mahdî will emerge in my ummah. He will live for five, or seven or nine. (Zayd – a narrator – doubted) Zayd says, 'We said, "What measurement is this of?" He ﷺ said, "Years." He ﷺ then said, "A person will come to him and say, 'O

114 'Aqâ'id e Islâm p.185

Mahdî, grant me, grant me."' He ﷺ said, "He will place so much (wealth) in his clothing that he will not be able to carry it."[115]

The famous *muhaddith*, Hadrat Maulânâ Rashîd Ahmad Gangohî رحمة الله عليه said the following in the light of this Hadîth, 'Once Rasûlullâh ﷺ gave the sahâbah glad-tidings of the goodness of the first three eras, they understood that trials and events would occur after that (the first three eras). There will be such a time after the best eras that every day will prove to be worse than the previous one.

The sahâbah رضي الله عنهم became worried about the future of the beloved *ummah* of Rasûlullâh ﷺ upon hearing this, that, what will be the condition of the *ummah* when they will be involved in religious works and death will come upon them suddenly? Also, who will awaken the *ummah* from the sleep of negligence in this time of evil, trials and deviation? Rasûlullâh ﷺ gave these glad-tidings in order to remove the worry of the sahâbah رضي الله عنهم so that they would be contented that even during this critical time, there will be emergence of guides. The emergence of guides is a clear proof that even in this era full of trials, the essence of goodness will be present and the teaching of *dîn* and the spread of the *Sunnah* will continue.'[116]

He further explains the reconciliation between the three figures narrated in this Hadîth, i.e. five, seven and nine,

فيعيش خمسا أو سبعا الخ ، والتوفيق بين هذه الروايات أن تجهيزه الجيش في

خمس سنين ، ثم محاربته مع الكفار سنتان ، ثم يعيش بعد ذلك سنتين ، فتلك

---

[115] Jâmi' at Tirmidhî vol.2 p.47

[116] Al Kaukab Ad Durrî vol.2 p.57

تسعة بأسرها ، وعلى هذا فالترديد في هذه الروايات ليس بشك من الراوي ، بل هو تنويع في الرواية" .

'The reconciliation between these narrations is that preparation of his army will take place in five years, then war will be waged with the non Muslims for two years, he will then rule for two years. In this way, there remains no contradiction between the words of the Hadîth.'

THE STATUS OF *MAHDÎ* IN RELIGION, THIS WORLD, AND THE HEREAFTER

1. The following is explained in a Hadîth,

لن تهلك أمة أنا في أولها ، وعيسى بن مريم في آخرها ، والمهدي في أوسطها.

كنز العمال ١٤/٢٦٦ رقم ٣٨٦٧١

That ummah will never be destroyed, at whose beginning I am, at whose ending will be Îsâ bin Maryam and whose middle period will have Mahdî among them.[117]

2. He (Hadrat Mahdî ﷺ) will be the final *khalîfah e râshid*.

3. He will be the final *mujaddid*.

4. He will reach the highest level of sainthood (*wilâyah*).

---

[117] Kanz ul 'Ummâl vol.14 p.266, Hadîth 38671

5. The following narration describes him to be one of the leaders in paradise,

عن أنس بن مالك رضي الله عنه قال : سمعت رسول الله صلى الله عليه وسلم

يقول : نحن ولد عبد المطلب سـادة أهـل الجنـة ، أنـا وحمـزة وعـلي وجعفـر

والحسن والحسين والمهدي . ابن ماجة ٣٠٠

Hadrat Anas bin Mâlik ؎ narrates that he heard Rasûlullâh ﷺ saying, "We, the progeny of 'Abdul Muttalib will be the leaders in paradise, myself, Hamzah, 'Alî, Ja'far, Hasan, Husayn and Mahdî."[118]

This narration is not among the fabricated narrations of *Sunan Ibn Mâjah*. There are *mutâbi'* (see footnote 58) narrations for it, as well as narrations that corroborate this one.

6. He will be blessed by Allâh ﷻ with great spiritual strength.

7. His status is directly below that of the *Khulafâ' e Râshidîn*.

Hadrat Maulânâ Muhammad Idrîs Kândehlawî رحمة الله عليه writes regarding this,

'Imâm Mahdî is the final *khalîfah e râshid* of the *ummah* of Rasûlullâh ﷺ. His status is after that of Hadrat Abû Bakr ؎ and Hadrat 'Umar ؎ according to majority of the *'ulemâ'*.'[119]

8. All the inhabitants of the heavens and the earth will love him.

---

[118] Sunan Ibn Mâjah p.300

[119] Al Qaul al Muhkam fî Nuzûl 'Îsâ bin Maryam, well known as Nuzûl e 'Îsâ wa Zuhûr e Mahdî

9. The first *salâh* that Hadrat 'Îsâ ﷺ will perform after his descent will be as a follower of Hadrat Mahdî ؓ. This is a form of honour for this *ummah.* (A distinguished person of this *ummah* behind whom a Nabî will perform *salâh*)

10. He will not be a *Nabî* or a *Rasûl. Wahî* will not come to him, and he will not claim *nubuwwah.* No one will believe him to be a *Nabî.*

We learn from this that the person who claims to be the *Mahdî* as well as a *Nabî* is a liar. (Similarly, all those that claimed to be the *Mahdî* until today are also liars)

11. Hadrat Mahdî ؓ will be the *khalîfah* and the ruler of the Muslims until the descent of Hadrat 'Îsâ ﷺ.

12. Hadrat 'Îsâ ﷺ will hold the status of leader *(amîr)* after his descent, and Hadrat Mahdî ؓ will hold the status of minister *(wazîr)*. They will consult with one another.

Hadrat Maulânâ Muhammad Yûsuf Ludhiyânwî رحمة الله عليه writes regarding this,

'Hadrat 'Îsâ ﷺ will be the *khalîfah* after his descent. This position of his is part of the creed of the Muslims. It is for this reason that Hadrat Mahdî ؓ will hand the matters of the *khilâfah* over to him after his descent and he (Hadrat Mahdî ؓ) will become one of his ministers. All the Muslims will obey him. For this reason, there will be no need for any claims, nor any election or selection.'[120]

---

[120] Al Mahdî wa Al Masîh p.21

REMAINING HIDDEN UNTIL HIS EMERGENCE

After the study of Ahâdîth we realize that the emergence of Hadrat Mahdî ☺ has been kept hidden until a specified time. When the time for his emergence comes, this secret will suddenly be opened for the people by Allâh ﷻ. It is also surprising to note that Hadrat Mahdî ☺ will not be acquainted with his status. This is learnt from the following narration,

عن علي رضي الله عنه قال : قال رسول الله صلى الله عليه وسلم : المهـدي منـا

أهل البيت يصلحه الله في ليلة . ابن ماجة ٢/٣١٠ مسند أحمد ١/١٠٦

Hadrat ʿAlî ☺ narrates that Rasûlullâh ﷺ said, "Mahdî will be from us, the Ahl al Bayt, Allâh will bless him with the capacity overnight."[121]

Shaykh ʿAbdul Ghanî Dehlawî ﵀ writes in the commentary of this Hadîth,

أى يصلحه الله في ليلة أى يصلحه للامـارة والخلافـة بغـاءة وبغتـة . أنجـاح

الحاجة

Allâh will bless him with the capacity to rule and hold the position of *khalîfah* suddenly overnight.[122]

---

[121] Sunan Ibn Mâjah vol.2 p.310, Musnad Ahmad vol.1 p.106
[122] Anjâh Al Hâjah

'Allâmah Ibn Kathîr ﷬ writes in the commentary of this Hadîth,

أيْ يتوب الله عليه ويوفقه ويلهمه ويرشده بعد أن لم يكن كذلك . النهاية في الفتن والملاحم ١/٣١

Allâh will bless him with His special favour and will grant him divine ability, thereby inspiring him with this reality and making him acquainted with his position of which he was unaware.[123]

The characteristics and good qualities of Hadrat Mahdî ﷺ will remain hidden and unknown until the time for his emergence. For this reason, none will recognize him. Once the time for his emergence comes, in His infinite power, Allâh ﷻ will create all the abilities within him to rule in a single night. Due to this, his being the *Mahdî* will become so clear and open that a simpleton will be able to recognize him easily. His emergence will be loved and adored by all because of the great trials that will be present at that time.

Hadrat Maulânâ Badr e 'Âlam Mîrthî ﷬ writes,

'A deep reality is opened up by means of this. And that is, some people in whose hearts *îmân* is weak will question, when Hadrat Mahdî ﷺ will have such open fame, then how can he remain unrecognized by the general populace and the elite? The reason for this is that it cannot be understood that people will be waiting for his emergence at the time of great calamities and troubles. However, this sentence, '*Allâh will bless him with the capacity overnight*' has solved this difficulty. Even though many people possess these qualities, his (Hadrat Mahdî ﷺ's) inner works and spirituality will remain hidden by the will of Allâh. This will remain until the time for his emergence comes, for then, his inner

---

123 An Nihâyah fî Al Fitan wa Al Malâhim vol.1 p.31

specialities will be brought out in the open in a single night. It is as though this is a manifestation of the power (of Allâh) that none will be able to recognize him before his emergence. Once the time comes, then through the power of Allâh ﷻ, all the abilities will be created in him overnight. After this, it will be open even to a blind person that he is the *Mahdî*.

Look at how the emergence of *Dajjâl* is proven from authentic Ahâdîth, but how much is this proven reality hidden just before his emergence? Since seeing that these incidents are to happen in an age full of trials, it is a *fitnah* on its own to desire the emergence of *Mahdî* and the presence of *Dajjâl* and delve into this subject.'[124]

WHEN WILL THE *MAHDÎ* EMERGE?

The emergence of Hadrat Mahdî ﷺ is greatly emphasized in the Ahâdîth. We have also been given definite information that after his emergence, the Muslim *ummah* will develop and prosper. At the same time, the exact year and month has not been specified.

The conditions of the Muslim *ummah* at that time can be gauged to a great degree from the Ahâdîth. From these Ahâdîth, it can be learnt that the time for his emergence is close.

[124] Tarjumân us Sunnah vol.4 pp.404-405

THE GENERAL CONDITION OF THE *UMMAH* WHEN THE TIME OF HIS EMERGENCE IS CLOSE

1. The earth would have been filled with oppression and tyranny.

2. The oppression will be so great that no place of refuge would be found. Hâkim رحمة الله عليه has transmitted the following narration in this regard,

عن أبي سعيد الخدري رضي الله عنه قال : قال رسول الله صلى الله عليه وسلم : ينزل بامتي بلاء شديد من سلطانهم حتى يضيق الأرض عنهم فيبعث الله رجلا من عترتي فيملا الأرض قسطا وعدلا كما ملئت ظلما وجورا الخ .

مستدرك حاكم

Hadrat Abû Sa'îd Al Khudrî رضي الله عنه narrates that Rasûlullâh ﷺ said, "Great difficulities will come upon my ummah from their rulers, until the earth will become straigtened upon them. Allâh will then send a person from my family who will fill the earth with justice and equity just as it was filled with oppression and tyranny."

3. People will be spitting at one another.

عن علي رضي الله عنه قال : لا يخرج المهدي حتى يبصق بعضكم في وجه بعض . منتخب كنز العمال ٣٣/٦

It is narrated from Hadrat ʿAlî ⬞ that he said, "*Mahdî* will not
appear until that time wherein you will be spitting in one
another's faces.[125]

According to the research of Muftî Nizâm ud Dîn Shâmzî
⬞, this Hadîth can be relied upon.[126]

4. Taking the name of Allâh ⬞ will be a crime deserving capital
punishment.

إذا قال الرجل "الله الله" قتل . مستدرك حاكم ٤/٥٥٤

When a person will say, 'Allâh, Allâh', he will be killed.[127]

5. The *ummah* will face many tests.

6. There will be great differences and earthquakes, i.e. very
troubled conditions.

7. *Dîn* will decline.

8. There will be a flood of *fitnah*.

9. The conditions will be such that the Muslims will say out of
hopelessness, 'Will *Mahdî* ever come?' i.e. people will lose hope
with regards to the emergence of Hadrat Mahdî ⬞.

---

[125] Muntakhab Kanz al ʿUmmâl vol.6 p.33

[126] ʿAqîdah Zuhûr e Mahdî p.70

[127] Mustadrak Hâkim vol.4 p.554

عن ابن عباس رضي الله عنه قال يبعث المهدي بعد أياس وحتى يقول الناس "لا مهدي" . الحاوي ٢/٧٦

It is narrated from Ibn ʿAbbâs ؓ that he said, "*Mahdî* will emerge after a state of hopelessness and the people will say, 'There is no *Mahdî*'.

10. The Satanic powers will have dominance in the world.

11. Crookedness would have been created in the hearts of the Muslims.

12. There will be no importance given to *dîn* or the *sharî ʿah*.

13. *H̲arâm* will be understood to be *h̲alâl*.

14. Good will be taken to be evil and evil will be taken to be good.

The conditions that will come over the *ummah* can be understood from the following H̲adîth,

عن ثوبان رضي الله عنه قال : قال رسول الله صلى الله عليه وسلم : يوشك الامم أن تداعى عليكم كما تداعى الاكلة إلى قصعتها ، فقال قائل : ومن قلة نحن يومئذ؟ قال : بل أنتم يومئذ كثير ، ولكنكم غثاء كغثاء السيل ولينزعن الله من صدور عدوكم المهابة منكم ، وليقذفن الله في قلوبكم الوهن ، فقال قائل : يا رسول الله وما الوهن؟ قال : حب الدنيا وكراهية الموت . أبو داؤد ٢/٥٩٠ رقم ٤٢٩٧

Hadrat Thaubân ❧ *narrates that Rasûlullâh* ❧ *said, "A time will come upon you in which nations will invite one another to attack you like people are invited to eat from the food cloth. (Those who partake of the meals surround the food cloth. Similarly, these groups of non-Muslims will surround the Muslims). The sahâbah* ❧ *asked, "O messenger of Allâh, will our numbers be very few on that day?" Rasûlullâh* ❧ *replied, "No, you will be in great numbers at that time, but, (with regards to dîn), you will be like the scum of the flood waters. Awe for you will leave the hearts of the enemies and you will fall prey to 'wahn'. A person asked, "What is wahn?' He* ❧ *said, "Love of this world and fear of death."*[128]

BIOGRAPHIC DETAILS OF THE *MAHDÎ*

NAME AND LINEAGE

The name of Hadrat Mahdî ❧ is Muhammad, son of 'Abdullâh. His family relation is to the *Ahl al Bayt*, i.e. the Banû Hâshim. His father's lineage is traced back to Hadrat Hasan ❧. He is therefore a *Hasanî Sayyid* from this side. He is traced back to Hadrat Husayn ❧ - the martyr of Karbala – from his mother's side, making him a *Husaynî Sayyid*.

In essence, the narrations regarding this differ. Some state that he is *Hasanî*, while others state that he is *Husaynî*. Imâm Abû Dâwûd ﷦ has recorded the following narration in his *Sunan*,

قال أبو داؤد : وحدثت عن هارون بن المغيرة ، قال : حـدثنا عمـرو بـن أبي

قيس ، عن شعيب بن خالد ، عن اسحق قال : قال علي رضي الله عنه ونظر إلى

---

[128] Sunan Abû Dâwûd vol.2 p.590, Hadîth 4297

ابنه الحسن فقال : "إن ابني هذا سيد ، كما سماه النبي صلى الله عليه وسلم وسيخرج من صلبه رجل يسمى باسم نبيكم صلى الله عليه وسلم" . أبو داؤد ٢/٥٨٩ رقم ٤٢٩٠

Hadrat ʿAlî ◌ is reported to have said, while looking at his son, Hasan, "This son of mine is a leader, just as Rasûlullâh ◌ called him a *Sayyid*. A person will be born from his progeny whose name will correspond to the name of your Nabî."

حدثنا الوليد ورشدين ، عن ابن لهيعة ، عن أبي قبيل ، عن عبد الله بـن عمـرو رضي الله عنه قال : يخرج رجل من ولد الحسين من قبل المشرق ، لـو استقبله الجبال لهدمها واتخذ فيها طرقا . أخرجه الحاكم وابن عـساكر كما في الحـاوي ٢/٦٦

Hadrat ʿAbdullâh bin ʿAmr ◌ is reported to have said, "A man from the progeny of Husayn will emerge from the east. Even if a mountain has to come his way, he will destroy it and make his path across."[129]

After studying these two apparent contradictions, read the two answers provided by the author of *Nibrâs*. He writes,

اختلف في أن المهدي من أولاد الحسن أو الحسين رضي الله عـنهما؟ والـراجح هو الأول ، كما رواه أبو داؤد عن علي رضي الله عنه. رقم الحديث ٤٢٩٠ . وجمع بعضهم بأنه من صلب حسني وبطن حسينية . نبراس ٣١٦

---

[129] Al Hâwî vol.2 p.66

Scholars are of differing views as to the lineage of Hadrat Mahdî رضي الله عنه. Some say that he is of the progeny of Hadrat Hasan رضي الله عنه, while others are of the view that he is from the progeny of Hadrat Husayn رضي الله عنه. The preferred view is that he is from the progeny of Hadrat Hasan رضي الله عنه. A narration of Hadrat ʿAlî رضي الله عنه, transmitted by Imâm Abû Dâwûd رحمة الله عليه corroborates this. Some scholars have reconciled the two views, stating that his father will be from the progeny of Hadrat Hasan رضي الله عنه and his mother will be from the progeny of Hadrat Husayn رضي الله عنه.

A point worthy of note:

Ibn al Qayyîm Al Jauzî رحمة الله عليه writes,

وفي كونه من ولد الحسن سر لطيف ، وهو أن الحسن ترك الخلافة لله . فجعل الله من ولده من يقوم بالخلافة الحق ، المتضمن للعدل الذي يملأ الارض . وهذه سنة الله في عباده أنه من ترك لأجله شيئا أعطاه الله أو أعطى ذريته أفضل منه . المنار المنيف لابن القيم الجوزية ١٥١ كذا قال المناوي في فيض القدير ٦/٢٧٩

There is a subtle point worthy of note in Hadrat Mahdî رضي الله عنه being from the progeny of Hadrat Hasan رضي الله عنه. That is, Hadrat Hasan رضي الله عنه stepped down from the *khilâfah* for the pleasure of Allâh تعالى. In lieu of this, Allâh تعالى has decreed a person to emerge from his progeny who will establish the true *khilâfah*. It will be so just that the earth would be filled with justice. It is the way of Allâh تعالى among His servants that he who leaves something for the pleasure of Allâh تعالى, Allâh تعالى will bless him or his children with something better.[130]

---

130 Al Manâr Al Munîf p.151, Fayd al Qadîr vol.6 p.279

Note: It is known from some narrations that H̲ad̲rat Mahdî ؓ will be from the progeny of H̲ad̲rat ʿAbbâs ؓ.

اللهم انصر العباس وولد العباس ثلاث . يا عم أما علمت أن المهدي من ولدك موفقا ، رضيا ، مرضيا . منتخب كنز العمال ٦/٣١

Rasûlullâh ﷺ said, "O Allâh, help ʿAbbâs and the children of ʿAbbâs. (He ﷺ said this thrice). O my uncle, do you not know that Mahdî will be from your progeny. He will be guided, pleased and will be pleased with."[131]

The compiler of *Kanz ul ʿUmmâl* states after recording this narration that the narrators in the chain are reliable. In some chains of this narration, Mu̲hammad bin Zakariyyâ Al Ghallâbî is found. He is not reliable. Some scholars have said that he used to fabricate A̲hâdîth.[132]

If this narration is accepted, then it is possible that Rasûlullâh ﷺ pointed to H̲ad̲rat ʿAbbâs ؓ for this reason that he was the sole elder of the family at that time. It is common to refer to the progeny of someone by linking them to the elders or responsible people of the family.

Note: In some books, it is stated that the name of the mother of H̲ad̲rat Mahdî ؓ is Âmina. We could not find a reliable source for this.

TITLE

His well-known title is *Mahdî,* meaning 'guided' (one who has received guidance to the truth from Allâh ﷻ and together with this, he becomes a means of guidance for others). Every pious,

---

131 Muntakhab Kanz ul ʿUmmâl vol.6 p.31
132 Al Mughnî vol.2 p.300

guided person who treads the straight path can be called *'Mahdî'* in accordance to the lexical implication of the word. However, as a definition of the *Ahl us Sunnah* (which in reality is the definition of the *sharî'ah*), *Mahdî* refers to that honourable personality whose emergence before Hadrat 'Îsâ ﷺ has been prophesized in *mutawâtir* (see footnote 50) Ahâdîth. In conditions of despair, he will bring hope. He will be a means of elevating the *ummah* on a global level. His special signs and recognizable conditions are explained in authentic Ahâdîth that have authentic chains of transmission. These signs cannot be applied to anyone besides this special *Mahdî*.

THE WORD *'IMÂM'* OR *''ALAYHI AS SALÂM'* TOGETHER WITH THE NAME OF *MAHDÎ*

THE WORD *'IMÂM'*

Some people use the word *'imâm'* with the name of Hadrat Mahdî ؓ. Some of our scholars have given permission for this. This permission is backed by sound proof as well. However, it is appropriate not to use the word upon the basis of *'saddan lil bâb'*.[133] This word should not be used as a technical definition for him, nor is it correct to use it upon the basis of its lexical meaning. The reason for this is that a doubt is created about bringing a shî'ite viewpoint into vogue. This viewpoint is that the twelve individuals whom the shî'as believe to be sinless are referred to with the title *'imâm'*. Therefore, there would be confusion in using

---

[133] *Saddan lil Bâb* is translated as closing the door, i.e. to institute such a ruling that will close the door in the face of other incorrect things (before they could occur). – [T]

the word *'imâm'* when considering the usage of it by the shiʿas. It will be better to leave it out. The reason for not using it upon the basis of its lexical meaning is that this word is not used even for people who are much higher in status than Hadrat Mahdî ﷺ, like the *khulafâ' e râshidîn.*

THE WORD *'ʿALAYHI AS SALÂM'*

Some people use the word *'ʿalayhi as salâm'* together with the title *Mahdî.* According to common usage *(ʿurf),* this is special with the messengers and the angels. Hadrat Mahdî ﷺ is neither a messenger, nor an angel. Therefore, the word *'ʿalayhi as salâm'* should not be used with his name. It is appropriate to use the word *'radiyallâhu anhu'* (ﷺ).

Subsequently, our honourable teacher, Hadrat Muftî Saʿîd Ahmad Pâlanpûrî writes in his unique commentary of *Hujjatullâh al Bâligha,* titled *Rahmatullâh al Wâsiʿa,*

Note: Hadrat Shâh Walîullâh رحمه الله has used the word *'ʿalayhi as salâm'* in his Friday sermons for Hadrat Hasan ﷺ and Hadrat Husayn ﷺ, whereas the belief of *imâmah* is that of the shîʿas. The reason put forward that it was possibly used in the lexical meaning is incorrect because this word was not used with the names of the *khulafâ' e râshidîn,* whereas they were more deserving of it. Similarly, many authors use the word *'ʿalayhi as salâm'*. This cannot be correct in any way according to the *ahl us sunnah* because the belief of *imâmah* and infallibility is that of the shîʿas.[134]

---

[134] Rahmatullâh al Wâsiʿa vol.1 p.85

Maulânâ Khayr Mu<u>h</u>ammad Jâlandharî رحمه الله عليه has written along similar lines in reply to a question recorded in *Khayr al Fatâwâ* vol.1 p.147.

In summary, *'Imâm Mahdî* عليه السلام*'* is an effect of shism that has become famous among people. It could also be said or written unknowingly out of intense love. It is necessary to refrain from it.

Whether it is correct or not to use the word *'ra<u>d</u>iyallâhu anhu'* remains to be discussed. To use the word *'ra<u>d</u>iyallâhu anhu'* after his emergence will be permissible in the light of the various narrations regarding him. One narration of *Kanz ul 'Ummâl* vol.14 p.270, <u>H</u>adîth 38586 is quoted below,

يرضي عنه ساكن السماء وساكن الأرض

The inhabitants of the skies and the earth will be pleased with him.

Note: The word *'Imâm'* has been used a lot in the *A<u>h</u>âdîth* for <u>H</u>a<u>d</u>rat Mahdî رضي الله عنه. It is for this reason that a great number of the early and contemporary scholars have been using the word *'Imâm'*. However, because the belief of *imâmah* is a foundational and important belief of the shî'as, it is appropriate for us to refrain from using it.

وللنّاس في ما يعشقون مذاهب

For people is that which their way loves

The summary of this discussion is that the appropriate title is <u>H</u>a<u>d</u>rat Mahdî رضي الله عنه.

PLACE OF ORIGIN

عن ام سلمة زوج النبي صلى الله عليه وسلم قال : "يكون اختلاف عند موت خليفة ، فيخرج رجل من أهل المدينة هاربا إلى مكة فيأتيه ناس من أهـل مكـة فيخرجونه وهو كاره فيبايعونه بين الركن والمقام الخ . أبو داؤد ٢/٥٨٩

Hadrat Umm e Salamah radiyallâhu anha - the wife of Rasûlullâh ﷺ - narrates that Rasûlullâh ﷺ said,"There will be difference of opinion upon the death of a khalîfah. A person will run from Madînah to Makkah. The people of Makkah will come to him to bring him out for imâmah, but he will dislike it. The people will then pledge allegiance to him at the place between Maqâm Ibrâhîm and the Hijr."[135]

The home and place of birth of Hadrat Mahdî ؓ is Madînah Munawwarah, and the place of his emergence is Makkah Mukarramah. He will migrate to *Bayt al Muqaddas* (in Shâm) with the objective of making *dîn* reign high. Mullâ ʿAlî al Qârî رحمة الله عليه writes in *Sharh Fiqh al Akbar,*

أن المهدي يظهر أولا في الحرمين الشريفين ، ثم يأتي بيت المقدس الـخ . شرح فقه الأكبر ١٣٦

Hadrat Mahdî ؓ will first emerge in the *Haramayn,* and then he will go to *Bayt al Muqaddas.*[136]

---

135 Sunan Abû Dâwûd vol.2 p.589

136 Sharh Fiqh al Akbar p.136

PHYSICAL FEATURES

Hadrat Shâh Rafi' ud Dîn Dehlawî رحمة الله عليه writes with regards to the physical features of Hadrat Mahdî رضي الله عنه,

'He will be moderately tall, his body will be agile, his colour will be clear and his face will be similar to that of Rasûlullâh ﷺ. His character will also resemble that of Rasûlullâh ﷺ to a complete degree.'[137]

The physical features of Hadrat Mahdî رضي الله عنه have been vaguely explained in the Ahâdîth together with his name and lineage. The reason for this is that there will be no confusion in identifying him. A narration of *Sunan Abû Dâwûd* about this is as follows,

عن أبي سعيد الخدري رضي الله عنه قال: قال رسول الله صلى الله عليه وسلم: المهدي مني أجلي الجبهة أقنى الأنف يملأ الأرض قسطا وعدلا كما ملئت ظلما وجورا ويملك سبع سنين. سنن أبو داؤد ٢/٥٨٨

Hadrat Abû Sa'îd al Khudrî رضي الله عنه narrates that Rasûlullâh ﷺ said,"The Mahdî will be from my progeny. He will have a wide forehead and a high thin nose. He will fill the earth with equity and justice just as it was filled with oppression and tyranny. He will rule for seven years."[138]

Two physical features of Hadrat Mahdî رضي الله عنه have been mentioned in this Hadîth for those who will see him. One is that he will have a luminous wide forehead. Second, he will have a high nose. Both of these show the beauty, elegance and handsomeness

---

[137] 'Alâmât e Qiyâmat p.10

[138] Sunan Abû Dâwûd vol.2 p.588

of man. This is why these two things were also found in the figure of Rasûlullâh ﷺ.[139]

The meaning of mentioning these two features should be taken that he (Hadrat Mahdî ﷺ) will be handsome and elegant. However, the basic sign by means of which he will be recognized is his works, that he will bring an end to oppression and tyranny. Our world will become a world of equity and justice.[140]

A narration of a similar nature is recorded in *Mustadrak Hâkim*,

عن أبي سعيد الخدري رضي الله عنه قال : قال رسول الله صلى الله عليه وسلم : المهدي منا أهل البيت أشم الأنف ، أقنى ، أجلى يملأ الأرض قسطا وعدلا كما ملئت جورا وظلما يعيش هكذا ، وبسط يساره واصبعين من يمينه المسبحة والإبهام وعقد ثلاثة . هذا حديث صحيح على شرط مسلم ، ولم يخرجاه .

مستدرك للحاكم ٤/٦٠٠ رقم ٨٦٧٠

Hadrat Abû Sa'îd al Khudrî ﷺ narrates that Rasûlullâh ﷺ said,"The Mahdî is from us – the Ahl al Bayt – his nose will be straight and long and his forehead will be wide. He will fill the earth with equity and justice just as it was filled with oppression and tyranny. He will live so many years." (After saying this) Rasûlullâh ﷺ (spreading his five fingers) opened his left hand and two fingers of his right hand (the index and thumb), keeping the other three closed. (He had seven fingers open in total).[141]

---

139 Shamâ'il e Tirmidhî p.2

140 Ma'ârif al Hadîth vol.8 p.171

141 Mustadrak Hâkim vol.4 p.600 Hadîth 8670

Some narrations explain the bodily features of Hadrat Mahdî ﷺ,

عن علي رضي الله عنه قال : المهدي فتى من قريش آدم ضرب من الرجال .
منتخب كنز العمال ٦/٣٤

It is narrated from Hadrat 'Alî ﷺ that he said, "The Mahdî is a young man from the *Quraysh,* of wheatish colour and his build will be thin and tall."[142]

Three of his bodily features are explained in the above texts. However, as far as his signs are concerned, this much is narrated that his life will resemble that of Rasûlullâh ﷺ. It cannot be denied that together with knowledge, practice, perfection in spirituality and character, his physical features will be a means of attracting and drawing people towards him.

Imâm Abû Dâwûd رحمة الله عليه has mentioned under the narration of Hadrat Umm e Salamah *radiyallâhu anha,*

يشبهه في الخُلق ولا يشبهه في الخَلق . أبو داؤد ٢/٥٨٩ رقم ٤٢٩٠

Hadrat Mahdî ﷺ will resemble Rasûlullâh ﷺ in character but not in physical features.[143]

The author of *Badhl ul Majhûd* writes,

(يشبهه في الخُلق) أى في أخلاقه العالية (ولا يشبهه في الخَلق) أى في ظاهر الصورة . بذل المجهود ٥/١٠٣

Hadrat Mahdî ﷺ will resemble Rasûlullâh ﷺ in lofty character but not in physical features.

---

142 Muntakhab Kanz ul 'Ummâl vol.6 p.34
143 Sunan Abû Dâwûd vol.2 p.589, Hadîth 4290

It also becomes clear that it is a great sign for the recognition of H̲ad̲rat Mahdî ﷺ for his character to resemble that of Rasûlullâh ﷺ. It is also known that it is not necessary that he resembles Rasûlullâh ﷺ completely in physical appearance.

THE EMERGENCE OF *MAHDÎ* AND GENERAL CONDITIONS OF THAT ERA AND HOW WILL THE EMERGENCE OF *MAHDÎ* TAKE PLACE?

We cannot specify the time of the emergence of H̲ad̲rat Mahdî ﷺ. However, many Ah̲âdîth mention the incidents surrounding his emergence. The summary of these narrations is that a *khalîfah* will pass away. There will be difference of opinion regarding the leadership, i.e. who should be made the leader. A capable person from Madinah Munawwarah (H̲ad̲rat Mahdî ﷺ, who would be until then unknown by the people) will go to Makkah Mukarramah. He will have the fear that people would make him the *khalîfah*. He will not like to accept the post of *khilâfah*. He will strive to keep himself hidden but the people of Makkah Mukarramah will recognize this handsome capable person. Despite him not wanting it, people will begin to pledge allegiance at his hands at the place between the *H̲ijr al Aswad* and *Maqâm Ibrâhîm*. The people who pledge allegiance at the blessed hands of H̲ad̲rat Mahdî ﷺ first will number three hundred and thirteen, corresponding to the number of participants in the battle of Badr and to the followers of T̲âlût ﷺ.[144] These three hundred and thirteen luminaries will have a very high level of *îmân* and they will be the best of all the people of every era after those of the *khayr al qurûn*[145]. Then, as the news will spread, the sincere ones will form different groups and join H̲ad̲rat Mahdî ﷺ. A group will come from the east and will help H̲ad̲rat Mahdî ﷺ in the establishment of his rule. The following narrations explain this,

حدثنا حرملة بن يحيى المصري وابراهيم بن سعيد الجوهري قالا : حدثنا أبـو صالح عبد الغفار بن داؤد الحراني قال : حدثنا ابن لهيعة ، عن أبي زرعة عمرو بن جابر الحضرمي ، عن عبد الله بن الحارث بن جزء الزبيـدي رضي الله عنـه قال : قال رسول الله صلى الله عليه وسلم : يخرج ناس مـن المشرق فيؤطـون للمهدي يعني سلطانه . سنن ابن ماجة ٣٠٠ رقم ٤٠٨٨

H̲ad̲rat ʿAbdullâh bin al H̲ârith bin Juz az Zabîdî ﷺ says that Rasûlullâh ﷺ said, "People will come from the east and help Hadrat Mahdî ﷺ."

After going into extensive detail with regards to the narrators of this H̲adîth, H̲ad̲rat Muftî Nizâm ud Dîn Shâmzî ﷺ says that this H̲adîth can be relied upon. This is because no one has classified it as *maud̲û* ʿ(see footnote 85).

---

144 According to the famous view, there were three hundred and thirteen s̲ah̲âbah ﷺ in the battle of Badr, and those who followed the guidance of H̲ad̲rat T̲âlût ﷺ and went forward to face Jâlût also numbered three hundred and thirteen.

145 The best of eras. They are the eras of Rasûlullâh ﷺ, the s̲ah̲âbah ﷺ and the tâbiʿîn. – [T]

The *Abdâl* from ʿIrâq, Shâm and Yemen will also come and pledge allegiance at the hands of H̲ad̲rat Mahdî ﷺ.

In the initial stages, the army of H̲ad̲rat Mahdî ﷺ will be ill-equipped. However, due to the blessings that will come from the help and assistance from Allâh ﷻ, he will progress.

أخبرنا عبد الرزاق ، عن معمر ، عن قتادة يرفعه إلى النبي صلى الله عليه وسلم قال : "يكون اختلاف عند موت خليفة ، فيخرج رجل من المدينة فيأتي مكة ، فيستخرجه الناس من بيته وهو كاره ، فيبايعونه بين الركن والمقام ، فيبعثه إليه جيش من الشام ، حتى إذا كانوا بالبيداء خسف بهم ، فيأتيه عصائب العراق وأبدال الشام ، فيبايعونه فيستخرج الكنوز ويقسم المال ، ويلقى الاسلام بجرانه الى الأرض ، يعيش في ذلك سبع سنين أو قال تسع سنين . مصنف عبد الرزاق ١١/٣٧١ رقم ٢٠٧٦٩ أبو داؤد رقم ٤٢٨٦

H̲ad̲rat Qatâdah ﷺ narrates that Rasûlullâh ﷺ said, "There will be difference of opinion after the demise of a khalîfah. A person will leave Madînah for Makkah. The people will take him out of his home and pledge allegiance at his hands at the place between the H̲ijr and Maqâm while he will dislike it. An army will be dispatched from Shâm to face him. When that army will reach Baydâ', it will be swallowed by the earth. Then groups from ʿIrâq and the Abdâl from Shâm will arrive and pledge allegiance at his hands. He will take out the treasures and distribute it. Islâm will be established in the earth and he will live in these conditions for seven or nine years."[146]

عن حفصة رضي الله عنها أنها سمعت النبي صلى الله عليه وسلم يقول: ليؤمن هذا البيت جيش يغزونه حتى إذا كانوا ببيداء من الأرض يخسف بأوسطهم ، وينادي أولهم آخرهم ثم يخسف بهم فلا يبقى إلا الشريد الذي يخبر عنهم فقال رجل أشهد عليك أنك لم تكذب على حفصة . وأشهد على حفصة أنها لم تكذب على النبي صلى الله عليه وسلم . مسلم ٢/٣٨٨ رقم ٢٨٨٣

Hadrat Hafsah radiyallâhu anha narrates that she heard Rasûlullâh ﷺ saying, "An army will definitely head for this house (the Baytullâh). When they reach Baydâ', the centre part of the army will be swallowed by the earth. The front part of the army will call out to the rear part of the army; the earth will swallow them too. None will be saved except the informant."[147]

حدثني محمد بن حاتم بن ميمون ، حدثنا الوليد بن صالح ، حدثنا عبيد الله بن عمرو ، أخبرنا زيد بن أبي انيسة ، عن عبد الملك العامري ، عن يوسف بن ماهك قال : أخبرني عبد الله بن صفوان ، عن ام المؤمنين رضي الله عنها أن رسول الله صلى الله عليه وسلم قال : سيعوذ بهذا البيت يعني الكعبة قوم

---

146 Musannaf 'Abdur Razzâq vol.11 p.371, Hadith 20769, Sunan Abû Dâwûd, Hadîth 4286

147 Sahîh Muslim vol.2 p.388, Hadîth 2883

ليست لهم منعة ولا عدد ولا عدة ، يبعث إليهم جيش حتى إذا كانوا ببيداء من الأرض خسف بهم . قال يوسف : وأهل الشام يومئذ يسيرون إلى مكة ، فقال عبد الله بن صفوان أم والله ما هو بهذا الجيش . قال زيد : وحدثني عبد الملك العامري ، عن عبد الله بن سابط ، عن الحارث بن أبي ربيعة ، عن أم المؤمنين بمثل حديث يوسف بن ماهك غير أنه لم يذكر فيه الجيش الذي ذكره عبد الله بن صفوان . مسلم ٢/٣٨٨

Umm al Mu'minîn ra<u>d</u>iyallâhu anha narrates that Rasûlullâh ﷺ said, "A nation that will not have the ability to defend themselves will seek protection at the Baytullâh. They will neither have the numbers nor will they be ready. An army will be dispatched to them (to face them). When this army reaches Baydâ', they will be swallowed by the earth." Yûsuf bin Mâhak – a narrator – says that the people of Shâm will march to Makkah at that time. [148]

THE EMERGENCE OF *SUFYÂNÎ* AND THE FIRST CLEAR MIRACLE OF <u>H</u>A<u>D</u>RAT MAHDÎ رضي الله عنه

The story of *Sufyânî* is a very important one when discussing the incidents relating to <u>H</u>a<u>d</u>rat Mahdî رضي الله عنه. *Sufyânî*[149] is related to the *Quraysh* and his maternal family is the *Banû Kalb*. For this reason, the people of *Banû Kalb* will rally around him.

---

[148] <u>Sa</u>hî<u>h</u> Muslim vol.2 p.388

[149] He will be from the progeny of Khâlid bin Yazîd bin Abû Sufyân. The title Sufyânî is derived from his lineage. His name will be ʿUrwah.

He will be from the desert part of Damascus in Shâm. He will move to the corners of Shâm and Egypt. *Sufyânî* is a great tyrant and oppressor who will kill infants. He will carry out general massacres, and the *Sâdât*[150] will be targeted the most. The bellies of women will be ripped open and their children will be killed. The tribe of *Qays* will gather against him but he will kill them all. The narrations explaining this are collected below,

عن أبي هريرة رضي الله عنه قال : قال رسول الله صلى الله عليه وسلم : يخرج رجل يقال له السفياني في عمق دمشق ، وعامة من يتبعه من كلب ، فيقتل حتى يبقر بطون النساء ويقتل الصبيان ، فتجمع لهم قيس فيقتلها حتى لا يمنع ذنب تلعة – ويخرج رجل من أهل بيتي في الحرة فيبلغ السفياني ، فيبعث له جندا من جنده ، فيهزمهم ، فيسير اليه السفياني بمن معه ، حتى إذا صار ببيداء من الأرض خسف بهم ، فلا ينجو منهم إلا المخبر عنهم . هذا حديث صحيح الاسناد على شرط الشيخين ، ولم يخرجاه . مستدرك على الصحيحين ٤/٥٦٥ رقم ٨٥٨٦

Hadrat Abû Hurayrah ﷺ narrates that Rasûlullâh ﷺ said, "A person called Sufyânî will come out from Damascus. Most of his followers will be of the Banû Kalb. He will kill to such an extent that he will rip the bellies of women and murder their children. The tribe of Qays will gather a force against him. He will kill them until no one will remain. Then a person of my family (Hadrat Mahdî ﷺ) will emerge from Hira. When this news will reach Sufyânî, he will send out one of his

150 The progeny of Rasûlullâh ﷺ. – [T]

armies. He (Hadrat Mahdî ﵇) will defeat them all. Sufyânî will then face him with his own army. When they (the army of Sufyânî) will reach Baydâ', the earth will swallow them. None of them will remain except the informant."[151]

The crux of this is that when this oppressive tyrannical person will hear of the emergence of Hadrat Mahdî ﵇, he will immediately send one of his armies to face Hadrat Mahdî ﵇. This army will head for Makkah Mukarramah and will encamp at *Baydâ'*.[152] Suddenly, the centre part of the army will sink into the earth. Those at the front of the army will inform those at the back so that they do not fall into the same predicament. However, before they can resort to any plan to save themselves, they will be sunken too. The sinking of this large army into the earth will be (a manifestation of) the help of Allâh ﷻ and it will be a miracle that will make Hadrat Mahdî ﵇ famous in far away lands.

عن عائشة رضي الله عنها قالت : قال رسول الله صلى الله عليه وسلم :
العجب أن ناسا من أمتي يؤمون البيت برجل من قريش قد لجأ بالبيت حتى
إذا كانوا بالبيداء خسف بهم ، فقلنا يا رسول الله : ان الطريق قد يجمع الناس ،
قال : نعم ! فيهم المستبصر والمجبور وابن السبيل ، يهلكون مهلكا واحدا
ويصدرون مصادر شتى ، يبعثهم الله على نياتهم. مسلم ٢/٣٨٨ رقم ٢٨٨٤

It is narrated from Hadrat 'Â'isha radiyallâhu anha that she said, "Rasûlullâh ﷺ said, 'It is surprising to note that a few people from my

---

151 Mustadrak 'alâ As Sahîhayn vol.4 p.565, Hadîth 8586

152 Baydâ' is a barren land in front of Dhul Hulayfah in the direction of Makkah Mukarramah

ummah will set out for the Baytullâh together with a person from the Quraysh who has taken protection in the Baytullâh. When they reach Baydâ', they will be sunk into the earth." We said, "O Messenger of Allâh, there will be all types of people on the path." Rasûlullâh ﷺ said, "Yes, among them will be people who are pleased, people who have been forced and travelers. They will all be destroyed at once. Allâh will then raise them up on the day of Qiyâmah according to their intentions."[153]

Note: When *Sufyânî* will hear of the sinking of the army, he will set out himself for Makkah Mukarramah. He will launch an attack on Makkah Mukarramah. Under the leadership of Ḥaḍrat Mahdî ☘, the Muslims will be very weak as far as equipment is concerned. It will be like the scene of Badr, but, the help of Allâh ﷻ will come and the army of *Sufyânî* would be heavily defeated. The army of Ḥaḍrat Mahdî ☘ will be victorious.

A narration transmitted by Imâm Abû Dâwûd رحمة الله عليه, narrated by Ḥaḍrat Umm e Salamah *raḍiyallâhu anha* with regards to this is quoted hereunder,

حدثنا محمد بن المثنى ، حدثنا معاذ بن هشام ، حدثني أبي ، عـن قتـادة ، عـن صالح أبي الخليل ، عن صاحب له ، عن أم سلمة زوج النبي صلى الله عليه وسلم قال : يكون اختلاف عند موت خليفة ، فيخرج رجل من أهـل المدينـة هاربا إلى مكة ، فيأتيه ناس من أهل مكة ، فيخرجونه وهو كاره ، فيبايعونه بين الركن والمقام ، ويبعث إليه بعث من الشام ، فيخسف بهم بالبيـداء بـين مكـة

---

153 Saḥîh Muslim vol.2 p.388, Ḥadîth 2884

والمدينة ، فإذا رأى الناس ذلك أتاه أبـدال الـشام وعـصائب أهـل العـراق ، فيبايعونه ، ثم ينـشؤ رجـل مـن قـريش أخوالـه كلـب فيبعـث إلـيهم بعثـا ، فيظهرون عليهم وذلك بعث كلب ، والخيبة لمن لم يشهد غنيمة كلـب فيقـسم المال ويعمل في الناس بسنة نبيهم صلى الله عليه وسلم ويلقى الإسلام بجرانه إلى الأرض ، فيلبث سبع سنين ، ثم يتوفى ويصلي عليه المسلمون . أبـو داؤد ٢/٥٨٩

Hadrat Umm e Salamah radiyallâhu anha - the wife of Rasûlullâh ﷺ - narrates that Rasûlullâh ﷺ said, "There will be difference of opinion upon the demise of a khalîfah. A person will then run from Madînah to Makkah. The people of Makkah will bring him out and pledge allegiance at his hands at the place between the Hijr and Maqâm Ibrâhîm while he will dislike it. An army will be sent from Shâm to face him. This army will be sunk into the earth at Baydâ' – which is between Makkah and Madînah. When people will see this unnatural occurrence, then the abdâl from Shâm and the pious from Irâq will come in groups and pledge allegiance at his hands. A person from the Quraysh whose maternal uncle is from Banû Kalb will emerge. He will lead an army against Hadrat Mahdî ؓ. They (the army of Hadrat Mahdî ؓ) will defeat them. That will be the army of Kalb. It will be a loss for those not present when the spoils of Kalb will be distributed. (Hadrat Mahdî ؓ) will distribute the spoils and will rule amongst the people in accordance to the sunnah of their Messenger ﷺ. Islâm will place its neck upon the earth (Islâm will gain dominance in the earth). This will remain for seven years. Then Hadrat Mahdî ؓ will pass away and the Muslims will perform the janâzah salâh over him."[154]

From the text 'from his companion', we learn that one narrator is *majhûl* (see footnote 77). However, this *majhûl* narrator is known from other chains. His name is ʿAbdullâh bin Hârith.

Note: After defeating *Sufyânî* and the tribe of *Kalb*, Hadrat Mahdî ﷺ will distribute the spoils of war. He will distribute it in accordance to the *sunnah* of Rasûlullâh ﷺ. The receipients will be given as much as they can carry.

The importance of the spoils of this war is highlighted in the Ahâdîth,

عن أبي هريرة رضي الله عنه مرفوعا : المحروم من حرم غنيمة كلب ولو عقالا ، والذي نفسي بيده لتباعن نسائهم على درج دمشق ، حتى ترد المرأة من كسر يوجد بساقها . مستدرك للحاكم رقم ٨٣٢٩

It is narrated from Hadrat Abû Hurayrah ﷺ[155] *that he said, "The deprived is he who is deprived of the spoils of Kalb, even if it be a ʿiqâl.*[156] *By the being in whose control my life is, their women will be sold on the road of Damascus. A woman will be returned due to a broken shin."*[157]

The summary of this discussion is that all the people who will be part of the receipients of the booty attained from the war

---

[154] Sunan Abû Dâwûd vol.2 p.589

[155] This narration is *marfûʿ*

[156] ʿIqâl refers to a cord used for hobbling the feet of a camel, or a headband made of camel's hair. – [T]

[157] Mustadrak of Hâkim, Hadîth 8329

with Kalb (even though it is a *iqâl*) will be very fortunate. The person who is not part of it will be considered to be deprived. It is as though the people of truth have been encouraged to participate in the battle against *Sufyânî* and his forces in the Hadîth. Besides the booty, the women of Kalb will be taken as slaves and will be sold on the road of Damascus. A woman from among them will be returned because of her shin being broken.

CONQUEST OF SHÂM

The fame and acceptance of Hadrat Mahdî 🕮 will become widespread after his emergence and the defeat of *Sufyânî* and his forces. The people of truth will come to him from different places in groups upon groups. He will go from Makkah Mukarramah to Madînah Munawwarah. After presenting himself at the grave of Rasûlullâh 🕮, he will proceed to Shâm. The Romans will be ruling Shâm at that time.

We deem it appropriate to quote a detailed narration of Hadrat 'Abdullâh bin Mas'ûd 🕮, in which the wars that will be fought under the leadership of Hadrat Mahdî 🕮 and other conditions are explained. Nu'aym bin Hammâd 🕮 has recorded it in his '*Al Fitan*' wherefrom 'Allâmah Suyûtî has mentioned it in his '*Jâmi' as Saghîr*'. Sayyed Barzanjî 🕮 has mentioned it as well in his '*Al Ishâ'a*'. The sequence of all the incidents regarding Hadrat Mahdî 🕮 is highlighted in this narration. Many parts of this narration are clearly corroborated in the *Sihâh* books.

عن عبد الله بن مسعود رضي الله عنه قال : يكون بين المسلمين وبين الروم هدنة وصلح ، حتى يقاتلوا معهم عدوا لهم ، فيقاسمونهم غنائمهم ، ثم ان الروم يغزون مع المسلمين فارس ، فيقتلون مقاتلتهم ويسبون ذراريهم ، فيقولُ الروم : قاسمونا الغنائم كما قد قاسمناكم ، فيقاسمونهم الأموال وذراري الشرك ، فيقول الروم : قاسمونا ما أصبتم من ذراريكم ، فيقولون : لا نقاسمكم ذراري المسلمين أبدا ، فيقولون غدرتم بنا فترجع الروم الى صاحبهم بالقسطنطينية فيقولون : ان العرب غدرت بنا ، ونحن أكثر منهم عددا ، وأتم منهم عدة ، وأشد منهم قوة ، فأمدنا نقاتلهم ، فيقول : ما كنت لأغدر بهم ، قد كانت لهم الغلبة في طول الدهر علينا ، فيأتون صاحب رومية فيخبرونه بذلك فيوجه ثمانين غاية ، تحت كل غاية اثنا عشر ألفا في البحر ، ويقول لهم صاحبهم : إذا رسيتم بسواحل الشام فأحرقوا المراكب لتقاتلوا عن أنفسكم فيفعلون ذلك ، ويأخذون أرض الشام كلها برها وبحرها ، ما خلا مدينة دمشق والمعتق ، ويخربون بيت المقدس – قال فقال ابن مسعود رضي الله عنه : وكم تسع دمشق من المسلمين ؟ قال : فقال النبي صلى الله عليه وسلم : والذي نفسي بيده لتتسعن على من يأتيها من المسلمين كما يتسع الرحم على الولد – قال : قلت : وما المعتق يا نبي الله ؟ قال : جبل بأرض الشام من حمص على نهر يقال لها الأرنط ، فتكون ذراري المسلمين في أعلى المعتق والمسلمين على نهر الأرنط ، والمشركون خلف نهر الأرنط يقاتلونهم صباحا

ومساء ، فاذا أبصر ذلك صاحب القسطنطينية وجه في البر الى قنسرين ستمائة ألف حتى تجيئهم مادة اليمن سبعين ألفا ، ألف الله قلوبهم بالإيمان ، معهم أربعون ألفا من حمير حتى يأتوا بيت المقدس فيقاتلون الروم فيهزمونهم ويخرجونهم من جند الى جند ، حتى يأتوا قنسرين وتجيئهم مادة الموالي ، قال : قلت وما مادة الموالي يا رسول الله ؟ قال : هم عتاقتكم ، وهو منكم قوم يجيئون من قبل فارس فيقولون تعصبتم يا معشر العرب ، لا نكون مع أحد من الفريقين أو تجتمع كلمتكم ، فتقاتل نزار يوما واليمن يوما والموالي يوما ، فتخرجون الروم الى العمق وينزل المسلمون على نهر يقال له كذا وكذا يعزى ، والمشركون على نهر يقال له الرقية وهو النهر الأسود ، فيقاتلونهم فيرفع الله تعالى نصره عن العسكرين وينزل صبره عليهما حتى يقتل من المسلمين الثلث ، ويفر الثلث ، ويبقى الثلث ، فأما الثلث الذين يقتلون فشهيدهم كشهيد عشرة من شهداء بدر يشفع واحد من شهداء بدر لسبعين ، وشهيد الملاحم يشفع لسبع مائة ، وأما الثلث الذين يفرون فانهم يفترقون ثلثة أثلاث ، ثلث يلحقون بالروم ويقولون : لو كان الله بهذا الدين من حاجة لنصرهم وهم مسلمة العرب بهراء وتنوخ وطيء وسليح — وثلث يقلن : منازل آبائنا وأجدادنا خير لا تنالنا الروم أبدا ، مروا بنا البدو وهم الأعرب ، وثلث يقول : ان كل شيء كاسمه ، وأرض الشام كاسمها الشؤم ، فسيروا بنا الى العراق واليمن والحجاز حيث لا نخاف الروم ، وأما الثلث الباقي بعضهم الى بعض

يقولون : الله الله دعوا عنكم العصبية ولتجتمع كلمتكم وقاتلوا عدوكم فانكم لن تنصروا ما تعصبتم ، فيجتمعون جميعا ويتبايعون على أن يقاتلوا حتى يلحقوا باخوانهم الذين قتلوا ، فاذا أبصر الروم الى من قد تحول اليهم ومن قتل ورأوا قلة المسلمين قام رومي بين الصفين معه بند في أعلاه صليب فينادي "غلب الصليب" فيقوم رجل من المسلمين بين الصفين ومعه بند فينادي "بل غلب أنصار الله ، بل غلب أنصار الله وأولياءه" فيغضب الله تعالى على الذين كفروا من قولهم "غلب الصليب" فيقول يا جبريل أغث عبادي فينزل جبريل في مائة ألف من الملائكة ويقول : يا ميكائيل أغث عبادي فينحدر ميكائيل في مائتى ألف من الملائكة ، ويقول يا إسرافيل أغث عبادي فينحدر إسرافيل في ثلاث مائة ألف من الملائكة وينزل الله نصره على المؤمنين وينزل بأسه على الكفار فيقتلون ويهزمون ويسير المسلمون في أرض الروم حتى يأتوا عمورية وعلى سورها خلق كثير يقولون : ما رأينا شيأ أكثر من الروم كم قتلنا وهزمنا وما أكثرهم في هذه المدينة وعلى سورها ، فيقولون : آمنونا على أن نؤدي إليكم الجزية ، فيأخذون الأمان لهم ولجميع الروم على أداء الجزية وتجتمع إليهم أطرافهم فيقولون : يا معشر العرب ان الدجال قد خالفكم الى دياركم ، والخبر باطل فمن كان فيهم منكم فلا يلقين شيأ مما معه فانه قوة لكم على ما بقي فيخرجون فيجدون الخبر باطلا ، ويثب الروم على ما بقي في بلادهم من العرب فيقتلونهم حتى لا يبقى بأرض الروم عربي ولا

عربية ولا ولد عربي إلا قتل ، فيبلغ ذلك المسلمين فيرجعون غضبا لله عز وجل فيقتلون مقاتلتهم ويسبون الذراري ويجمعون الأموال ، لا ينزلون على مدينة ولا حصن فوق ثلثة أيام حتى يفتح لهم ، وينزلون على الخليج ويمد الخليج حتى يفيض فيصبح أهل القسطنطينية يقولون : الصليب مد لنا بحرنا والمسيح ناصرنا فيصبحون والخليج يابس فتضرب فيها الأخبية ويحسر البحر عن القسطنطينية ويحيط المسلمون بمدينة الكفر ليلة الجمعة بالتحميد والتكبير والتهليل إلى الصباح ليس فيهم نائم ولا جالس ، فاذا طلع الفجر كبر المسلمون تكبيرة واحدة فيسقط ما بين البرجين ، فتقول الروم ، إنما كنا نقاتل العرب فالآن نقاتل ربنا وقد هدم لهم مدينتنا وخربها لهم ، فيمكثون بأيديهم ويكيلون الذهب بالأترسة ويقتسمون الذراري حتى يبلغ سهم الرجل منهم ثلث مائة عذراء ، ويتمتعوا بها في أيديهم ما شاء الله ، ثم يخرج الدجال حقا ويفتح الله القسطنطينية على يد أقوام هم أولياء الله يرفع الله عنهم الموت والمرض والسقم حتى ينزل عليهم عيسى بن مريم عليه السلام فيقاتلون معه الدجال – الفتن ٣٢٣ الجامع الكبير ١٥/٢٣٨ رقم ١٣٥١٥

Hadrat Abû Hurayrah ﷺ narrates that Rasûlullâh ﷺ said[158]*, "There will be a truce between the Muslims and the Romans (Christians). Then the Muslims and Romans will jointly war against an enemy of the Romans. They will be victorious and distribute the booty amongst*

---

[158] The translation of this narration is not word for word. The understood meaning is presented here. – [T]

themselves. Then, the Romans together with the Muslims will fight against the Persians. They will kill their soldiers and imprison their children. The Romans will tell the Muslims, "Divide the booty equally between us this time just like we divided it the first time." The Muslims will divide the wealth and polytheist slaves (but not the Muslim slaves). The Romans will say that the Muslim captives should also be divided. The Muslims will say, "We shall never divide the Muslim captives." The Romans will say, "This is treachery."

The Romans will complain of this to the king of Constantinople, saying that the Muslims have betrayed us (You should therefore help us). We are much better off than the Muslims in numbers, wealth and strength. The king of Constantinople will tell them that he cannot betray the Muslims. They have been over us for a very long time. Finally, the Romans will go and complain to the king of Rome. He will send an army over sea of eighty flags, under each flag will be twelve thousand soldiers (totaling nine hundred and sixty thousand). The officers of this army will command the soldiers to burn their ships upon reaching the shores of Shâm so that they will fight for their lives. The soldiers will obey. The Christian Romans will conquer the entire Shâm except for Damascus and Mount Mu'taq. They will also destroy Bayt al Muqaddas.

In reply to a question posed by Ḥaḍrat 'Abdullâh bin Mas'ûd ؓ Rasûlullâh ﷺ said, "The Muslims will be great in number at that time in Damascus, and Mu'taq is a mountain near the river of Ḥims."

The scene could be drawn thus: the Muslim children will be at the top of Mu'taq, the Muslims will be based at the river Arnaṭ and the polytheists will be behind the river Arnaṭ. The armies will be on the edge of war morning and evening. When the king of Constantinople will see this, he will send an army of six hundred thousand by road to Qinnasarîn. A Yemeni army of seventy thousand *will join the Muslims. Forty thousand people of the Himyar tribe will join the Yemenis. Allâh would have joined their hearts through îmân. These people will come to Bayt al Muqaddas and fight the Romans. They will finally defeat them and destroy them completely, (after this) they will reach Qinnasarîn.*

An army of freed slaves (from Persia) will come to help the Arabs. They will say, "O Arabs, abandon tribalism. We shall never be able to help one another until we unite." Sometimes the Arabs, at other times, the Yemenis, while at other times, these slaves will fight the non Muslims. The Muslims will expel them to the farthest valleys. The Muslims will gather at a river and will be involved in finding out information from one another. The polytheists will gather at Nahr Ruqya. This river is also called Nahr Aswad. The Muslims will then fight the polytheists but Allaah will take victory away from the Muslims and bless them with patience. A third of the Muslim army will be martyred, a third will run away and a third will remain.

Every martyr of this army will earn the reward of ten martyrs of Badr. A martyr of Badr will intercede for seventy people and the martyrs of these wars of the final era will be permitted to intercede for seven hundred people.

The third that ran away will also be split into three parts. One part of them will turn renegade and join the Romans. They will say that if Allâh is in need of this dîn, then He will look after it Himself. These people will be the Arabs from Hirâ', Tannûkh, Tay' and Salîh. One third will be Bedouins. They will leave for their dwellings saying that the land of our ancestors is better for us. The Romans will never be able to reach us. One third will say that the name of everything has an effect on it. That is why this land of Shâm is unfortunate just like its name is. We will go to 'Irâq, Yemen and Hijâz where we shall have no fear of the Romans.

The third that remained will then say that definitely we should unite and leave out tribalism. We should fight the enemy as a united army. This tribalism is a barrier in the way of our success.

They will then fight with this vision that now we shall meet our martyred brothers. The Roman army will realize the small numbers of the Muslims that a third has been killed; a third has become part of us and only the last third remains. One person will stand, taking the flag of the cross, and say, "The cross has conquered." A Muslim will then take the flag and shout from between the two rows, "The helpers of Allâh have conquered."

Allâh will be angered at this statement of the Romans and will help the Muslims with six hundred thousand angels. One hundred thousand will be under Jibrîl, two hundred thousand will be under Mîkâ'îl and three hundred thousand will be under Isrâfîl. Allâh will help the Muslims and exact His vengeance upon the non-Muslims. The non-Muslims will be very badly defeated and the survivors will taste defeat disgracefully.

The Muslims will then enter Shâm and reach a place called 'Ammûriyya. Many people will be gathered at the borders of 'Ammûriyya. The Muslims will be very surprised when they see the vast number of Romans. 'How many did we not kill? How many were chased away defeated, yet we witness this scene of so many Romans in 'Ammûriyya and the surrounding areas. These people will seek amnesty from the Muslims by paying Jizya. The Muslims will be happy with their proposal and give protection to all the Romans. The Romans of the surrounding areas will spread the rumour that Dajjâl has emerged in your homeland. This news will be false. Rasûlullâh ﷺ advised those who will remain behind at that time not to leave any booty taken from the Romans behind because it would help them in the coming battles. The Muslims will leave (based on that rumour).

They will only come to know later that the news was false. The Romans will fall upon the remaining Muslims and exterminate them. No Arab man or woman will remain. The Romans will wipe out the entire generation of Arabs. Once the Muslims come to know of this, they will be angered and will return. They will fight them a second time. This time, the Muslims will kill the Roman soldiers and capture their families and children. The Muslims will gather all their wealth and goods. Allâh will bless them with victory over every city or fort they pass within three days. When the Muslims will reach the bay, the banks will overflow. The Christians will say upon witnessing this, "The banks have overflowed through the blessing of the cross in order to save us and our saviour is Masîh (Hadrat Îsâ عليه السلام)."

When morning arrives, they will see that the water has dried up. It has changed course for the sea at Constantinople. They will immediately encamp there. The Muslims will surround the city of kufr and will spend the night of Jumu'ah in reciting tahmîd, takbîr, and tahlîl. No one will sleep or sit. All the Muslims will sound takbîr once in the morning. One side of the city will fall. In a state of bewilderment, the Romans will say, "Our war was with the Muslims at first. Now, we have to face the Sustainer of the universe directly. He has destroyed our entire city for the Muslims."

The Muslims will wait a while and will then distribute the spoils of war using golden shields and filling them up. The families and children will also be distributed. (The women will be so many that) three hundred women will fall in the share of a single person. The Muslims will benefit from this booty until an appointed time.

Dajjâl will then emerge in reality. Constantinople will be conquered at the hands of such pious servants of Allâh who will remain healthy. No one will fall ill, nor will any sickness trouble them, until Îsâ ﷺ will descend. They will fight Dajjâl (and his Jewish army) together with Îsâ ﷺ."

Different pronounciations of certain words in this narration:

Mu ́taq, with a *tâ*. The name of a mountain.[159] Some narrations have *Mu ́naq,* with a *nûn*.[160] Others have it as *Mu ́iq,* with a *yâ*. *Arnat,* with a *nûn*.[161] Some narrations have the word as *Arît,* with a *yâ*.[162]

'Ammûriya, a city of the Roman Empire.[163]

There is great difference of opinion about the number of angels that will descend to help the Muslims in this war. In *Al Fitan* and *Al Ishâ 'a,* Hadrat Jibrîl ﷺ, Hadrat Mîkâ'îl ﷺ and Hadrat Isrâfîl ﷺ are mentioned. In *Al Jâmi 'al Kabîr* only Hadrat Jibrîl ﷺ and Hadrat Mîkâ'iil ﷺ are mentioned. In addition, some narrations state three hundred thousand while others state six hundred thousand.

Note: It is quite probable that some portions of this narration are quite surprising. It should be remembered that the debated narrators of this particular narration, i.e. Ibn Lahî'ah, Hârith A'war and Muhammad bin Thâbit are the cause for the status of it being *da 'îf* (see footnote 83). However, note that a lot

---

[159] Mu'jam al Buldân of Hamawî vol.8 p.286

[160] Al Fitan of Nu'aym bin Hammâd رحمه الله

[161] Ibid

[162] Al Jâmi' al Kabîr vol.15 p.238, Al Qâmûs

[163] Mu'jam al Buldân vol.6 p.355

that was mentioned in it is corroborated by authentic Ahâdîth as was already explained.

We present a few narrations of *Sahîh Muslim* in this regard,

عن أبي هريرة رضي الله عنه أن رسول الله صلى الله عليه وسلم قال: "لا تقوم الساعة حتى تنزل الروم بالأعماق أو بدابق، فيخرج إليهم جيش من المدينة من خيار أهل الأرض يومئذ، فإذا تصافوا قالت الروم: خلوا بيننا وبين الذين سبوا منا نقاتلهم، فيقول المسلمون: لا، والله لا نخلي بينكم وبين إخواننا، فيقاتلونهم فينهزم ثلث لا يتوب الله عليهم أبدا، ويقتل ثلث هم أفضل الشهداء عند الله، ويفتح الثلث لا يفتنون أبدا. فيفتتحون قسطنطينية فبيناهم يقتسمون الغنائم قد علقوا سيوفهم بالزيتون إذ صاح فيهم الشيطان أن المسيح قد خلفكم في أهليكم، فيخرجون وذلك باطل فإذا جاءوا الشام خرج، فبيناهم يعدون للقتال يسوون الصفوف إذ أقيمت الصلوة، فينزل عيسى بن مريم صلى الله عليه وسلم فأمهم، فإذا رآه عدو الله ذاب كما يذوب الملح في الماء، فلو تركه لانذاب حتى يهلك، ولكن يقتله الله بيده، فيريهم دمه في حربته". مسلم ٢/٣٩٢ رقم ٢٨٩٧

Hadrat Abû Hurayrah ﵁ narrates that Rasûlullâh ﷺ said, "Qiyâmah will not happen until the Romans have not encamped in A'mâq or Dâbiq.[164] *An army comprising of the best Muslims residing*

---

[164] Two cities close to Aleppo and Antioch in Shâm

*on earth at that time will leave for Madînah. When they stand in
battle formation, the Romans will say, "Leave us and our captives to
fight with those whom we have collectively taken captive." The
Muslims will say, "Never, by Allâh, we shall not leave you to fight our
brothers." They will then fight. A third of the Muslim army will run
away. Allâh will never forgive them. Another third will be martyred.
They will be the greatest martyrs in the sight of Allâh. The final third
will be victorious. These victors will never become involved in any
fitnah or calamity. They will conquer Constantinople. They will hang
their swords on olive trees and will be distributing the spoils when
suddenly Shaytân will let out a scream that Dajjâl has reached your
homes in your absence.[165] They will leave everything and depart.
When they reach Shâm, Dajjâl would have emerged. They will be
forming their ranks in preparation for fighting when the time for ṣalâh
will come in. Îsâ ﷺ[166] will descend from the heavens and lead them in
ṣalâh. The enemy of Allâh (Dajjâl) will dissolve upon his sight as salt
dissolves in water. If he has to leave him, he will dissolve on his own
and be destroyed. However, Allâh will kill him at the hands of Îsâ
who will then show the people the blood of Dajjâl on his spear."[167]*

The reason for the breaking of the treaty and war between
the Muslims and Romans in the narration of Nuʿaym bin
Ḥammâd رحمه الله and *Saḥîḥ Muslim* can be understood in brief from
a previous battle in which the Muslims and Romans jointly
defeated the Persians. They will have differing views concerning

---

[165] This will be false

[166] According to common usage, the sentence ﷺ is reserved for the *Ambiyâ'*.
However, Rasulullâh ﷺ used it after the names of the *Ambiyâ'* on various
occasions. – [T]

[167] Saḥîḥ Muslim vol.2 p.392, Ḥadîth 2897

the distribution of the slaves attained as booty. This is because there will be some Muslims among the Persian captives. They would have either accepted Islâm after the war or they would have been Muslims from before and had to participate in the war against the Muslims due to governmental reasons.

A narration of Hadrat ʿAbdullâh bin Masʿûd ﷺ about the details of the conquest of Shâm in *Sahîh Muslim* is presented forthwith,

عن يسير بن جابر قال : هاجت ريح حمراء بالكوفة فجاء رجل ليس له هجيرى إلا "يا عبد الله بن مسعود جاءت الساعة ؟" قال فقعد وكان متكئا ، فقال : " ان الساعة لا تقوم حتى لا يقسم ميراث ولا يفرح بغنيمة ، ثم قال بيده هكذا ونحاها نحو الشام فقال : عدو يجمعون لأهل الشام ويجمع لهم أهل الإسلام ، قلت : الروم تعنى ؟ قال : نعم ، قال : ويكون عند ذاكم القتال ردة شديدة ، فيشترط المسلمون شرطة للموت لا ترجع إلا غالبة فيقتتلون حتى يحجز بينهم الليل ، فيفىء هؤلاء وهؤلاء كل غير غالب وتفنى الشرطة ، ثم يشترط المسلمون شرطة للموت لا ترجع إلا غالبة فيقتتلون حتى يحجز بينهم الليل ، فيفىء هؤلاء وهؤلاء كل غير غالب وتفنى الشرطة ، ثم يشترط المسلمون شرطة للموت لا ترجع إلا غالبة فيقتتلون حتى يمسوا ، فيفىء هؤلاء وهؤلاء كل غير غالب وتفنى الشرطة ، فإذا كان اليوم الرابع نهد إليهم بقية أهل الاسلام ، فيجعل الله الدائرة عليهم ، فيقتتلون مقتلة إما قال لا يرى مثلها وإما قال : لم ير مثلها حتى أن الطائر ليمر بجنباتهم فما يخلفهم

حتى يخر ميتا ، فيتعاد بنو الأب كانوا مائة فلا يجدونه يقى منهم إلا الرجل الواحد ، فأبى غنيمة يفرح أو أى ميراث يقاسم ...الخ" مسلم ٢/٣٩٢ رقم ٢٨٩٩

Hadrat Yasîr bin Jâbir says that once there was a strong red hurricane in Kûfa. A person whose expletive was, '*Qiyâmah* has come' came to Hadrat ʿAbdullâh bin Masʿûd ﷺ and asked, "Has *Qiyâmah* come?" Hadrat ʿAbdullâh bin Masʿûd ﷺ replied, "*Qiyâmah* will not happen until the distribution of inheritance does not stop and there will be no joy upon booty." He ﷺ then indicated towards Shâm and said, "The enemy will gather to fight the Muslims and the Muslims will gather to fight the enemy." The narrator says that I asked, "Do you mean the Christians by 'the enemy'?" Hadrat ʿAbdullâh bin Masʿûd ﷺ said, "Yes." He ﷺ then said, "At the onset of this war, there will be great losses. A portion of the Muslim army will go forward on the condition that they will be martyred or will return victorious. They will fight until night will separate them. No one will return victorious and the Muslims will be martyred. The Muslims will send forth another part of the army on the condition that they will be martyred or will return victorious. They will fight until nightfall. No one will return victorious and this part of the Muslim army will also be martyred. The Muslims will send another part of the army on the condition that they will be martyred or will return victorious. They will fight until evening. No one will return victorious and the Muslims will be martyred.

The rest of the Muslims will stand and face them on the fourth day and Allâh will defeat the enemy. This is because a war of this nature will never been seen (or ʿAbdullâh bin Masʿûd ﷺ

said), such a war has never been seen. It will be to such a degree that a bird will fly across the corpses and will die before passing them all.

When the members of a family will count his family, he will find only one percent of them left (or one person will be left). So, with which booty will he be happy with and whose inheritance will he distribute?..."

Note: Even though the Romans will be in control of most of the areas of Shâm, but the Muslims will still have control over certain areas (most probably, Damascus and the surrounding areas). There will be Roman captives with the Muslims as well. Certain narrations mention that the Roman army that will be in Shâm will be of seventy flags. Every flag will have twelve thousand soldiers under it, totaling eight hundred and forty thousand. This is one calculation. Other narrations mention other amounts.

Review the following narrations of Hadrat ʿAuf bin Mâlik ﷺ,

عن عوف بن مالك رضي الله عنه مرفوعا في حديث طويل ، فيه "ثم هدنة تكون بينكم وبين بني الأصفر ، فيغدرون فيأتونكم تحت ثمانين غاية ، تحت كل غاية اثنا عشر ألفا " صحيح البخاري ١/٤٥١

Hadrat ʿAuf bin Mâlik ﷺ narrates in a lenghthy marfû ʿHadîth that there will be a truce between you and Banû al Asfar. They will break it and come to you with an army comprising eighty flags. There will be twelve thousand soldiers under each flag.

عن عوف بن مالك رضي الله عنه مرفوعا في حديث طويل ، فيه "والسادسة هدنة تكون بينكم وبين بني الأصفر ، فيسيرون إليكم على ثمانين غاية ، قلت : وما الغاية ؟ قال : الراية ، تحت كل راية اثنا عشر ألفا ، فسطاط المسلمين يومئذ في أرض يقال لها الغوطة في مدينة يقال لها دمشق" . أحمد . حسب ترتيب الفتح السرباني ٢٤/٢٤،٢٥

Hadrat 'Auf bin Mâlik ﷺ narrates in a lenghthy marfû 'Hadîth that there will be a truce between you and Banû al Asfar. They will come to you under eighty flags. Each flag will have twelve thousand soldiers under it. The Muslims will be encamped at that time in a place called Ghautah which is in Damascus."[168]

The Roman army totals nine hundred and sixty thousand in the light of the two above-mentioned narrations.

Hadrat Mahdî ﷺ will head for the Christian headquarters where majority of the population are Christians, in Rome, Italy after the conquest of Shâm.

---

[168] Ahmad vol.24 pp.24,25

CONQUEST OF CONSTANTINOPLE[169]

'Allâmah Ibn Jarîr Tabarî رحمة الله عليه writes in his unique exegesis of the Qur'ân under the following verse,

وَمَنْ أَظْلَمُ مِمَّن مَّنَعَ مَسَاجِدَ اللّٰهِ أَن يُذْكَرَ فِيهَا اسْمُهُ وَسَعَىٰ فِي خَرَابِهَا أُوْلَـٰئِكَ مَا كَانَ لَهُمْ أَن يَدْخُلُوهَا إِلاَّ خَآئِفِينَ لَهُمْ فِي الدُّنْيَا خِزْيٌ وَلَهُمْ فِي الآخِرَةِ عَذَابٌ عَظِيمٌ

Who can do greater wrong than the one who prevents the name of Allâh from being taken in the Masâjid (he prevents others from salâh and from dhikr) and who does all he can to destroy them? (There can be no worse evil) Such people may only enter them (the Masâjid) in fear (unable to repeat their wrong). For them shall be disgrace (humiliation) in this world and a terrible punishment in the Âkhirah.
[Sûrah al Baqarah (the Bull) 2:114]

'The verse refers to the Romans that destroyed *Bayt al Muqaddas.*'

He writes further, in the commentary of 'For them shall be disgrace in this world', 'this refers to the conquest of Constantinople at the hands of (Hadrat Mahdî) رضي الله عنه and the killing of the Romans.'[170]

After conquering Europe, Hadrat Mahdî رضي الله عنه will head for Constantinople. It is assumed that the Christians would have seized and taken control of Constantinople. Constantinople is a city like an island. From the various Ahâdîth, we assume that Constantinople will be surrounded by walls when the emergence

---

[169] Modern day Istanbul, Turkey
[170] Tafsîr Tabarî vol.1 p.548

of Hadrat Mahdî ☀ takes place. The narrations of *Sahîh Muslim* that detail the conquest of Constantinople are presented here,

عن أبي هريرة رضي الله عنه أن النبي صلى الله عليه وسلم قال : "هل سمعتم بمدينة جانب منها في البر وجانب في البحر ، قالوا : نعم يا رسول الله ، قـال : لا تقوم الساعة حتى يغزوها سبعون ألفا من بني اسحق ، فإذا جاءوها نزلوا ، فلم يقاتلوا بسلاح ولم يرموا بسهم ، قالوا لا إله إلا الله والله أكبر فيسقط أحد جانبيها ، قال ثور : لا أعلمه إلا قال : الذي في البحر ، ثم يقولون الثانية لا إله إلا الله والله أكبر فيسقط جانبها الآخر ، ثم يقولون الثالثة لا إلـه إلا الله والله أكبر فيفرج لهـم ، فيـدخلونها فيغنمـوا ، فبينما يقتسمون المغـانم إذ جاءهم الصريخ فقال : إن الدجال قد خرج ، فيتركون كل شئ ويرجعون" . مسلم ٢/٣٩٦ رقم ٢٩٢٠

Hadrat Abû Hurayrah ☀ narrates that Rasûlullâh ☀ said, "Have you heard of a city, one side of which is (joined) to the land and the other side is in the sea?" The sahâbah ☀ replied, "Yes." Rasûlullâh ☀ then said,"Qiyâmah will not happen until seventy thousand Muslims of Banû Ishâq or Banû Ismâ îl war on it. When the Muslims arrive there and encamp, they will not fight with weapons, nor will they shoot any arrows. They will call out, 'There is none worthy of worship but Allâh and Allâh is the greatest' and one of the city walls will fall." Thaur – a narrator – says, "According to what I remember, it is the walls of the side in the sea." "The Muslims will then call out, 'There is none worthy of worship but Allâh and Allâh is the greatest' upon which the second city wall will fall. Upon the third call of 'There is no diety but Allâh and Allâh is the greatest', the path for the Muslims will be clear and they will enter victorious. They will be distributing the booty when Shaytân will shout that Dajjâl has emerged. The Muslims will leave everything and return to their homes (for protection)."[171]

Note: According to some scholars of Hadîth, *'seventy thousand from Banû Ishâq'* in reality refers to *Banû Ismâ îl*. All the copies of *Sahîh Muslim*, however, have the word *Banû Ishâq*.

Imâm Nawawî رحمة الله عليه writes,

قال القاضي : كذا هو في جميع أصول صحيح مسلم "من بني اسحق" قال : قال بعضهم : المعروف المحفوظ "من بني اسمعيل" وهو الذي يدل عليه الحديث وسياقه لأنه إنما أراد العرب وهذه المدينة هي القسطنطينية . نووي على هامش مسلم ٢/٣٩٦

Qâdî says, "The like is narrated in all the copies of *Sahîh Muslim*, i.e. *Banû Ishâq*. However, the famous and relied upon implication is *Banû Ismâ îl* because the meaning of the Hadîth points to this. This is also the demand of the context of the Hadîth because it implies Arabs. The 'city' mentioned in the Hadîth is Constantinople.

This interpretation could also be presented regarding using *'Banû Ishâq'* to refer to *'Banû Ismâ îl'* that in accordance to the proverb, *'the uncle of a man is his father's twin'*, it is correct to link a person to his uncle.

If we take the literal meaning of the Hadîth, then *Banû Ishâq* would refer to those individuals who accepted Islâm and

---

171 Sahîh Muslim vol.2 p.396, Hadîth 2920

joined the army of Hadrat Mahdî ﷺ, as is learnt from the previous narrations.

We learn from the various narrations that verification of the rumours regarding the emergence of *Dajjâl* will be taken very seriously, to such an extent that Hadrat Mahdî ﷺ will appoint a special group for this task. Note the following Hadîth,

فيبعثون عشر فوارس طليعة . قال رسول الله صلى الله عليه وسلم إني لأعرف أسمائهم وأسماء آبائهم وألوان خيولهم ، هم خير فوارس على ظهر الأرض يومئذ ، أو (قال) من خير فوارس على ظهر الأرض يومئذ . صحيح مسلم ٢/٣٩٢ رقم ٢٨٩٩

Mahdî will send a brigade of ten horsemen to verify the news. Rasûlullâh ﷺ said, "I know their names, their fathers' names and the colour of their horses. They will be the best riders on earth at that time."[172]

They will come to know that the news was false. However, when Hadrat Mahdî ﷺ will reach Shâm with his army, then *Dajjâl* would have emerged. Consequently, a Hadîth states,

فإذا جاءوا الشام خرج . صحيح مسلم ٢/٣٩٢ رقم ٢٨٩٩

When they reach Shâm, he would have emerged.[173]

Note: In the course of all these conquests, Hadrat Mahdî ﷺ will go to the Vatican. The great treasures that the Ceaser of Rome seized when conquering *Bayt al Muqaddas* are kept here. In his time, the Ceaser of Rome took and transported the treasure using one hundred and seventy thousand wagons.

---

[172] Sahîh Muslim vol.2 p.392, Hadîth 2899

[173] Ibid

Hadrat Mahdî ﷺ will take the treasure to *Bayt al Muqaddas* loading it upon one hundred and seventy thousand ships. It is at this place where Allâh ﷻ will gather the entire creation, from the first to the last.[174]

THE DESCENT OF HADRAT ʿÎSÂ عليه السلام AND THE DEMISE OF HADRAT MAHDÎ ﷺ

THE DESCENT OF HADRAT ʿÎSÂ عليه السلام THE DEMISE OF HADRAT MAHDÎ ﷺ AND THE GENERAL CONDITION OF THAT ERA

From amongst the signs of *Qiyâmah,* the descent of Hadrat ʿÎsâ عليه السلام deserves great importance. This subject is so vast and important that where the scholars of Hadîth have recorded separate chapters on this subject, other people of knowledge have written on it as well.

It is appropriate to mention a few important incidents in sequence very consisely that will happen upon the descent of Hadrat ʿÎsâ عليه السلام. This is so that a clear picture of the works and status of Hadrat Mahdî ﷺ during the era of Hadrat ʿÎsâ عليه السلام in the light of reliable narrations and historical reports can be before us.

Dajjâl will first emerge between ʿIrâq and Syria. However, his emergence will not be famous among people at that time. He will then show himself in Yahûdiyya, Isfahân. Here, his fame will spread. He will create *fitnah* in all four directions.

---

[174] For details, see At Tadhkira lil Qurtubî p.653, Tafsîr e Qurtubî vol.10 p.222

There are various places for the emergence of *Dajjâl* mentioned in the Ahâdîth. A central valley of Shâm and ʿIrâq, Khurâsân, Hauz wa Kirmân and Isfahân are mentioned.

A narration of *Sahîh Muslim* mentions a valley of ʿIrâq and Shâm,

عن نواس بن سمعان رضي الله عنه مرفوعا أنـه (الـدجال) خـارج خلـة بـين الشام والعراق . صحيح مسلم ٢/٤٠١ رقم ٢٩٣٧

It is narrated from Hadrat Nawwâs bin Samʿân ﷺ in a marfûʿ narration that Dajjâl will emerge from a central valley of ʿIrâq and Shâm.

Khurâsân is mentioned in a narration of Hadrat Abû Bakr Siddîq ﷺ, recorded in *Al Fath ar Rabbânî,*

عن أبي بكر رضي الله عنه قال : حـدثنا رسـول الله صـلى الله عليـه وسـلم أن الدجال يخرج من أرض بالمشرق يقال لها خراسان . الفتح الرباني ٢٤/٧٣

Hadrat Abû Bakr Siddîq ﷺ narrates that Rasûlullâh ﷺ said that Dajjâl will emerge from a land in the East called Khurâsân.

A narration of Hadrat Anas bin Mâlik ﷺ in *Al Fath ar Rabbânî* mentions Isfahân,

عن أنس بن مالك رضي الله عنه قال : قال رسول الله صلى الله عليـه وسـلم : يخرج الدجال من يهودية أصبهان . الفتح الرباني ٢٤/٧٣

Hadrat Anas bin Mâlik ﷺ narrates that Rasûlullâh ﷺ said, "Dajjâl will emerge from Yahûdiyya, Isfahân."

We find mention of Hauz wa Kirmân in *Al Fath ar Rabbânî* narrated by Hadrat Abû Hurayrah ﷺ,

عن أبي هريرة رضي الله عنه قال : سمعت رسول الله صلى الله عليه وسلم :
يخرج الدجال حوزوكرمان . الفتح الرباني ٢٤/٧٣

Hadrat Abû Hurayrah ﷺ narrates that he heard Rasûlullâh ﷺ saying, "Dajjâl will emerge in Hauz wa Kirmân."

The first three of the above quoted narrations are authentic. However, a narrator of the fourth – Muhammad bin Ishâq is a *mudallis*[175]. This is a cause for *du'f*[176] in it.

Reconciliation of the different places can be done in this way that the emergence of *Dajjâl* will be at first from a central valley of 'Irâq and Shâm. At that time, he will not be famous because a large group of his helpers will be waiting for him in Yahûdiyyah. He will then proceed to Yahûdiyyah in Isfahân, a city of Khurâsân. Together with his helpers, he will travel the entire world. In order to attain his objectives, he will settle at Hauz wa Kirmân. From the wording of the following Hadîth, we come to know that Hauz wa Kirmân will be the place where *Dajjâl* will settle,

لينزلن الدجال حوزوكرمان

He will settle at Hauz wa Kirmân

His emergence and evil will become famous when he comes out this time.

---

[175] A *Mudallis* is a narrator that narrates from a person living in the same time as him in such a way that people think that he has met and heard the one he narrates from, but he did not meet or hear from that person. [Irshâd Usûl ul Hadîth p.92] – [T]

[176] Weakness – [T]

Now *Dajjâl* will make a whirlwind travel of the earth. He will live on earth for forty days. One day will be like a year, the second day will be like a month and the third day will be like a week. The rest of the days will be normal.

Most of the followers of *Dajjâl* will be Jews. Hadrat Mahdî ﵁ will begin preparations for battle when he reaches Damascus. However, conditions will be in favour of *Dajjâl* because he will have great inherent strength. Hadrat Mahdî ﵁ and those who want him will stay in Damascus and will be engaged in preparation for battle. They will generally perform their *salâh* in the Jâmiʿ Umawî.

In this era of *fitnah,* the Muslims will gather in Jordan and *Bayt al Muqaddas*. At first, the Muslims will be in Ufayq, a valley of Jordan. The following is mentioned in *Musannaf Ibn Abî Shaybah,*

فينحاز (المسلمون) إلى عقبة أفيق . مصنف إبن أبي شيبة ١٥/١٣٧

The Muslims will withdraw to the valley of Ufayq.[177]

We come to know from certain narrations that all those who believe in Allâh ﷻ and the Day of *Qiyâmah* will be located in that valley of Jordan.

وكل واحد يؤمن بالله واليوم الآخر ببطن الاردن . كنز العمال ١٤/٣١٤ رقم ٣٨٧٩١ مستدرك حاكم ٤/٥٣٧ رقم ٨٥٠٧

All those who believe in Allâh and the Day of *Qiyâmah* will be in the valley of Jordan.[178]

---

177 Musannaf Ibn Abî Shaybah vol.15 p.137

178 Kanz ul ʿUmmâl vol.14 p.315, Hadîth 38791, Mustadrak Hâkim vol.4 p.537, Hadîth 8507

The Muslims will finally gather at a mountain in Jerusalem, *Jabal ad Dukkhân.*

On the other side, *Dajjâl* will cause disorder in the entire world and come to Damascus. He will encamp on the side of the mountain and surround a group of Muslims.

فيفر الناس إلى جبل الدخان وهو بالشام ، فيأتيهم فيحاصرهم ، فيشد حصارهم ، ويجهدهم جهدا شديدا . التذكرة للقرطبي ٧٥٤ أحمد ٣١٧،٣١٨/٤

The people will run to *Jabal ad Dukkhân* in Shâm. *Dajjâl* will come there and surround them. He will put them through great difficulty.[179]

The Muslims will be put through great difficulty and poverty due to this siege of *Dajjâl.* Some people will burn the strings of their bows and eat it. When the siege of *Dajjâl* will become very long, then the leader of the Muslims (Hadrat Mahdî ﵁), will say, "Why are you hesitant in fighting this rebel?" He will encourage them for victory or martyrdom. After the *Fajr salâh,* this decisive army will make a resolute intention (to go to battle – [T]).

This night will be very dark. The people will be involved in battle preparations. In this dark morning, Hadrat Mahdî ﵁ would have already stepped forward to lead the *Fajr salâh* while the Muslims are still preparing for *salâh.* The *iqâmah* would already be called out, when suddenly a sound will be heard saying, 'Your helper has arrived.'

The Muslims will be looking in every direction. Their sight will fall upon Hadrat 'Îsâ ﵇ who will be descending upon

---

[179] At Tadhkira lil Qurtubî p.754, Ahmad vol.3 pp.317-318

the white minaret of the Jâmi' Masjid of Damascus. He will be dressed in two yellow sheets with his hands on the shoulders of two angels. Hadrat 'Îsâ ﷺ will request for a ladder and descend from the minaret.

فبينما هو كذلك إذ بعث الله المسيح بن مريم ، فنزل عند المنارة البيضاء شرقي دمشق بين مهرودتين واضعا كفيه على أجنحة ملكين . التذكرة للقرطبي ٧٠٢

The Muslims will be in this condition when suddenly, Allâh will send Al Masîh bin Maryam ﷺ upon the eastern white minaret of Damascus. He will have his hands placed on the shoulders of two angels.[180]

The group of Muslims upon whom Hadrat 'Îsâ ﷺ will descend will be the most pious group of men and women on earth at that time.[181]

عن أبي هريرة رضي الله عنه أن رسول الله صلى الله عليه وسلم قال : ينزل عيسى بن مريم على ثمان مائة رجل وأربع مائة امرأة خيار من على الأرض يومئذ وكصلحاء من مضى . كتاب التذكرة ٧٦٢ كنز العمال رقم ٣٨٨٦٣

Hadrat Abû Hurayrah ﷺ narrates that Rasûlullâh ﷺ said, "Îsâ bin Maryam will descend among eight hundred men and four hundred women. They will be the best of those on earth at that time and they will be of a status similar to the pious people of before."[182]

Hadrat Mahdî ﷺ will call Hadrat 'Îsâ ﷺ in order to lead the *salâh* and he will leave the front place and move backwards.

---

[180] At Tadhkira lil Qurtubî p.702

[181] According to one narration, the men will number eight hundred and the women four hundred.

[182] Kitâb ut Tadhkira p.762, Kanz ul 'Ummâl, Hadîth 38863

Hadrat ʿÎsâ ﷺ will place his hand on the back of Hadrat Mahdî ﷺ and say, "You should lead the *salâh* because the *iqâmah* was called out for you." He ﷺ will refuse the position of *imâmah* and will say, "It is an honour for this *ummah* that some are leaders over the others."

عن أبي أمامة رضي الله عنه – مرفوعا – فرجع ذلك الامام ينكص يمشي القهقرى ليتقدم عيسى يصلي بالناس ، فيضع عيسى يده بين كتفيه ثم يقول له : تقدم فصل فإنها لك أقيمت . ابن ماجة رقم ٤٠٧٧

In a *marfû* ʿ(see footnote 53) narration, *Hadrat Abû Umâmah* ﷺ *relates, "This Imâm will turn and walk backwards so that Îsâ can come forward and lead the people in salâh. Îsâ will place his hand between his (Hadrat Mahdî ﷺ's) shoulders and then say, "Go forward and perform the salâh for the iqâmah was called out for you."*[183]

The *salâh* of this time will be lead by Hadrat Mahdî ﷺ and Hadrat ʿÎsâ ﷺ will perform *salâh* behind him.

At this point, it should be remembered that the opposite has been narrated with regards to *imâmah* from Hadrat Abû Hurayrah ﷺ,

عن أبي هريرة رضي الله عنه قال : سمعت رسول الله صلى الله عليه وسلم يقول : ينزل عيسى عليه السلام فيؤمهم . سعاية عن ابن حبان ٢/١٨٤

Hadrat Abû Hurayrah ﷺ narrates, "I heard Rasûlullâh ﷺ saying, " Îsâ ﷺ will descend (and will) then lead them (in salâh)."[184]

---

[183] Sunan Ibn Mâjah, Hadîth 4077

[184] Siʿâyah vol.2 p.184 from Ibn Hibbân

Similarly,

فينزل عيسى عليه السلام فأمهم . صحيح مسلم ٢/٣٩٢ رقم ٢٨٩٧

'Îsâ ﷺ will descend (and will) then lead them (in salâh).[185]

'Allâmah Kashmîrî رحمة الله عليه writes in clarifying the apparent contradiction,

'Hadrat 'Îsâ ﷺ will perform the first salâh behind Hadrat Mahdî ﷺ, because the iqâmah would have been called out for him."[186]

The following explanation is mentioned in *'Âridatul Ahwadhî,*

قد روى أنه يصلي وراء امام المسلمين خضوعا لدين محمد صلى الله عليه وسلم وشريعته واتباعا واسخانا لأعين النصارى واقامة الحجة عليهم . عارضة الأحوذي ٩/٧٨

It is narrated that he will perform salâh behind the leader of the Muslims, humbling himself before the *dîn* of Muhammad ﷺ, and becoming a follower of it. One of the reasons for this is that the Christians will themselves witness this and it will stand as proof against them.[187]

Hâfiz Ibn Hajar 'Asqalânî رحمة الله عليه writes,

وفي صلاة خلف رجل من هذه الامة مع كونه في آخر الزمان وقرب قيام الساعة دلالة للصحيح من الأقوال ، أن الأرض لا تخلو عن قائم لله بحجة . فتح الباري ٦/٦١١

---

[185] Sahîh Muslim vol.2 p.392, Hadîth 2897

[186] Fayd al Bârî vol.4 pp.46-47

[187] vol.9 p.78

In the performance of <u>s</u>*alâh* behind a person from this *ummah* is a clear proof that this world will never be free of a person who will establish the commands of Allâh, although this incident is one of the final eras close to *Qiyâmah*.[188]

After this first <u>s</u>*alâh*, <u>H</u>a<u>d</u>rat 'Îsâ عليه السلام will become the *imâm* and <u>H</u>a<u>d</u>rat Mahdî رضي الله عنه will follow him. This is proven from a narration of <u>H</u>a<u>d</u>rat Ka'b رضي الله عنه,

عن كعب رضي الله عنه مرفوعا ...قال : فينظرون فإذا بعيسى بن مريم ، قال : وتقام الصلوة فيرجع امام المسلمين المهدي ، فيقول عيسى : تقدم فلك اقيمت الصلوة ، فيصلي بهم ذلك الرجل تلك الصلوة ، قال : ثم يكون عيسى اماما بعده . الفتن ٣٩٣ رقم ١٣٣٦

<u>H</u>a<u>d</u>rat Ka'b رضي الله عنه narrates – in a *marfû'* (see footnote 53) narration – *"The people will be looking, suddenly Îsâ bin Maryam will be descending. At that time, the <u>s</u>alâh will be commencing and the leader of the Muslims, Mahdî, will be walking backwards. Îsâ will say, "Go forward, the iqâmah was called out for you." This person (<u>H</u>a<u>d</u>rat Mahdî رضي الله عنه) will lead them in this <u>s</u>alâh. He said, " Îsâ will then be the imâm."*[189]

Mulla 'Alî al Qârî رحمه الله writes in *Shar<u>h</u> Fiqh al Akbar*,

الأصح أن عيسى يصلي بالناس ، ويقتدي به المهدي . شرح فقه الأكبر ١٣٧

The correct view is that (after the first <u>s</u>*alâh*) 'Îsâ will lead the people in <u>s</u>*alâh* and *Mahdî* will follow him.[190]

---

188 Fat<u>h</u> al Bârî vol.6 p.611

189 Al Fitan p.393, <u>H</u>adîth 1336

190 p.137

After the *Fajr salâh,* there will be a lengthy discussion and consultation. After this, the war against *Dajjâl* and his followers will begin.

When *Dajjâl* will see Hadrat 'Îsâ عليه السلام, he will be shocked and will stand up and run. There will be approximately seventy thousand Jews with him. *Dajjâl* will run from Damascus to Isra'îl. He will pass the valley of Ufayq and reach the city of Ludd. However, the army of Hadrat 'Îsâ عليه السلام and Hadrat Mahdî رضي الله عنه will follow them. When *Dajjâl* will try to enter Ludd, then Hadrat 'Îsâ عليه السلام will come close to him. The condition of *Dajjâl* will be such that even if Hadrat 'Îsâ عليه السلام does not do anything, then too, *Dajjâl* will dissolve like salt and will be destroyed. Hadrat 'Îsâ عليه السلام will kill him with his weapons. The followers of *Dajjâl* will also be killed.

After (finishing off – [T]) *Dajjâl,* Hadrat 'Îsâ عليه السلام and Hadrat Mahdî رضي الله عنه will turn their attention to conquering the rest of the world and will establish Islâm in the entire world. Allâh ﷻ will make Islâm dominant in every way. The prophesy of Rasûlullâh ﷺ mentioned in the following Hadîth will be realized,

عن المقداد رضي الله عنه أنه سمع رسول الله صلى الله عليه وسلم يقول : لا يبقي على ظهر الأرض بيت مدر ولا وبر إلا أدخله الله كلمة الإسلام بعز عزيز وذل ذليل ، اما يعزهم الله فيجعلهم من أهله أو يذلهم فيدينون لها . قلت : فيكون الدين كله لله . أحمد ٣٩/٢٣٦ رقم ٢٣٨١٤

Hadrat Miqdâd رضي الله عنه narrates that he heard Rasûlullâh ﷺ saying, "No home made of baked bricks or unbaked bricks will remain on earth except that Allâh will place the word of Islâm in it. Some will be honoured and some will be disgraced. Those whom Allâh wishes to honour, He will bless them with the divine ability to become Muslims on their own, and those whom Allâh wishes to disgrace, they will finally choose Islâm." I said, "Then the entire dîn will be for Allâh."[191]

The summary of this discussion is that Hadrat Mahdî ﷺ will war against the Christians in different battles for seven years. He will fight against *Dajjâl* in the eighth year, and he will pass the ninth year together with Hadrat 'Îsâ ﷺ. At that time, Islâm will be flourishing in the entire world. Wealth will also be in great abundance. After the killing of *Dajjâl,* Hadrat Mahdî ﷺ will travel the earth together with Hadrat 'Îsâ ﷺ. They will also give glad-tidings of reward and will console those who were given great difficulty by *Dajjal.* They will also fill the hearts of the people by means of beneficience.

DEMISE OF HADRAT MAHDÎ ﷺ

The most authoritative information with regards to the demise of Hadrat Mahdî ﷺ is that he will not be martyred in any battle. In the ninth year after his emergence (according to one report), he will pass away at the age of forty-nine. No information could be found concerning the city in which he will pass away and where he will be buried. Only this much is mentioned in the following narration of *Sunan Abû Dâwûd,*

ثم يتوفى ويصلي عليه المسلمون . سنن أبو داؤد ٢/٥٨٩ رقم ٤٢٨٦

He will pass away and the Muslims will perform the *janâzah salâh* over him.[192]

Al 'Aun Al Ma'bûd, commentary of *Sunan Abû Dâwûd,* states the following about the narrators of the above narration,

---

[191] Ahmad vol.39 p.236, Hadîth 23814

[192] Sunan Abû Dawûd vol.2 p.589, Hadîth 4286

ورجاله رجال الصحيحين لا مطعن فيهم ولا مغمز . ١١/٢٥٥

This narration is narrated by narrators of the S̲ah̲îh̲ayn and there is no scope for *jarh̲*[193] and *t̲a'n*[194] on them.[195]

'Allâmah Anwar Shâh Kashmîrî رحمة الله عليه says in *Al 'Arf ush Shadhî,*

ويبعث المهدي لإصلاح المسلمين ، فبعد نزول عيسى عليه السلام يرتحل المهدي من الدنيا إلى العقبى . العرف الشذي على هامش جامع الترمذي ٢/٤٧ حسب النسخة الهندية

H̲ad̲rat Mahdî رضي الله عنه will be sent for the reformation of the Muslims. After the descent of H̲ad̲rat 'Îsâ عليه السلام, he (H̲ad̲rat Mahdî رضي الله عنه) will move from this world to the hereafter.[196]

It seems most apparent that the *janâzah s̲alâh* of H̲ad̲rat Mahdî رضي الله عنه will be performed by H̲ad̲rat 'Îsâ عليه السلام. It is accepted that H̲ad̲rat Mahdî رضي الله عنه will live for nine years after his emergence. He will be forty years of age at the time of his emergence. This is written in different books but we could not find an authentic narration proving this. Some *d̲a'îf* (see footnote 83) narrations do specify these numbers of years.

---

[193] *Jarh̲* means 'wound'. In the study of H̲adîth it refers to the scrutiny of a narration and the negative grading or statement made about it. – [T]

[194] *Ta'n* means 'to throw a spear, to find fault.' In H̲adîth terminology, it refers to the discussion regarding the reliability of a narrator, his memory and his religious practice. [Irshâd Us̲ûl ul H̲adîth p.98] – [T]

[195] vol.11 p.255

[196] vol.2 p.47

أخرج أبو نعيم ، عن أبي أمامة رضي الله عنه مرفوعا ... فقال لـه رجـل : يـا

رسول الله من امام الناس يومئذ؟ قال صلى الله عليه وسلم : المهدي من ولدي

ابن أربعين سنة الخ . الحاوي ٦٦/٢

Abû Nu'aym ؓ has transmitted the following *marfû* (see footnote 53) narration of Ḥaḍrat Abû Umâmah ؓ,

A person said, "O Messenger of Allâh, who will be the leader of the Muslims on that day?" Rasûlullâh ﷺ replied, "Mahdî, who is from my progeny. He will be forty years of age at that time."[197]

BRIEF BIOGRAPHY OF ḤAḌRAT 'ÎSÂ ؑ

After the demise of Ḥaḍrat Mahdî ؓ, Ḥaḍrat 'Îsâ ؑ will handle all the government affairs. Ḥaḍrat 'Îsâ ؑ will live in the world for forty years. He will marry and have children. The incident of *Yajûj* and *Mâjûj* will occur in his time. He will finally appoint a successor named Muq'ad before leaving this world, i.e. after this person is born, Ḥaḍrat 'Îsâ ؑ will pass away. He will be buried near Rasûlullâh ﷺ in the *rauḍah*. The final signs of *Qiyâmah* will then occur.

قال كعب الأحبار : ان عيسى عليه السلام يمكـث في الأرض أربعـين سـنة ،

وقال : وان عيسى عليه السلام يتـزوج بـامرأة مـن آل فـلان ، ويـرزق منهـا

ولدين فيسمى أحدهما محمدا والآخر موسى ، ويكون الناس معـه عـلى خـير

وفي خير زمان ، وذلك أربعين سنة ، ثم يقبض الله روح عيسى ويذوق الموت

---

[197] Al Ḥâwî vol.2 p.66

ويدفن إلى جانب النبي صلى الله عليه وسلم في الحجرة ، ويموت خيار الأمة ويبقى شرارها في قلة من المؤمنين . التذكرة للقرطبي ٧٦٣

Hadrat Ka'b Ahbâr رحمة الله عليه says that Hadrat 'Îsâ عليه السلام will live in the world for forty years. He will marry a woman from one of the tribes. This woman will bear him two sons whose names will be Muhammad and Mûsâ. The people will be together with him in goodness and in the good era. This will be a period of forty years. Allâh تعالى will then take the soul of Hadrat 'Îsâ عليه السلام. In this way, death will also come upon Hadrat 'Îsâ عليه السلام. He will be buried next to Rasûlullâh ﷺ in the blessed room. The pious of the *ummah* will pass away and the evil people will remain among very few Muslims.[198]

A verse of the Taurâh about this has been narrated from Hadrat 'Abdullâh bin Salâm رضي الله عنه,

عن يوسف بن عبد الله بن سلام عن أبيه قال : نجد في التوراة أن عيسى بن مريم يدفن مع محمد صلى الله عليه وسلم . الفتن ٣٩٥ رقم ١٣٣٨

It is narrated from Yûsuf bin 'Abdullâh bin Salâm from his father, "We found in the Taurâh that 'Îsâ bin Maryam will be buried with (next to) Rasûlullâh ﷺ."[199]

The following narration of *Musnad Ahmad* and *Musannaf Ibn Abî Shaybah* proves that Hadrat 'Îsâ عليه السلام will live in the world for forty years,

---

[198] At Tadhkira lil Qurtubî p.763

[199] Al Fitan p.359, Hadîth 1338

عن عائشة رضي الله عنها قالت : قال رسول الله صلى الله عليه وسلم : يخرج الدجال وينزل عيسى فيقتله ثم يمكث عيسى في الأرض أربعين عاما اماما عادلا وحكما قسطا . مسند أحمد رقم ٢٤٤٦٧ مصنف ابن أبي شيبة ١٥/١٣٤ رقم ١٩٣٢٠

Hadrat Â'isha radiyallâhu anha narrates that Rasûlullâh ﷺ said, "Dajjâl will emerge and Îsâ will descend. He (Îsâ) will kill him and will then live in the earth for forty years as a just ruler and an impartial judge."[200]

عن أبي هريرة رضي الله عنه قال : قال رسول الله صلى الله عليه وسلم : ينزل عيسى بن مريم ويقتل الدجال ويمكث أربعين عاما يعمل فيهم بكتاب الله تعالى وسنتي ويموت ويستخلفون بأمر عيسى رجلا من بني تميم يقال له المقعد ، لم يأت على الناس ثلث سنين حتى يرفع القرآن من صدور الرجال ومصاحفهم . الحاوي ٢/٨٢

Hadrat Abû Hurayrah ؓ narrates from Rasûlullâh ﷺ, "Îsâ bin Maryam will descend and he will kill Dajjâl and he will live in the earth for forty years. He will implement the book of Allâh and my Sunnah. He will pass away and will leave a person from Banû Tamîm named Muq'ad as his successor. In less than three years, the Qur'ân will be lifted from the hearts of people and from the Masâhif."[201]

---

[200] Musnad Ahmad, Hadîth 24467, Musannaf Ibn Abî Shaybah vol.15 p.134, Hadîth 19320

[201] Al Hâwî vol.2 p.82

Note: Study our book, *'Nuzûl e Îsâ'* for the complete biography of Hadrat 'Îsâ ﷺ, his descent and the killing of *Dajjâl.*

Finally, when Allâh ﷻ will establish *Qiyâmah,* he will create a pleasing breeze that will (be a cause – [T]) for taking the souls of all the believers. No believer will remain on earth. *Qiyâmah* will then happen on the worst of people and the trumpet will be blown.

عن عبد الله بن عمرو بن العاص رضي الله عنه ... ثم يبعث الله ريحا كريح المسك مسها مس الحرير ، فلا تترك نفسا في قلبه مثقال حبة من الإيمان إلا قبضته ، ثم يبقى شرار الناس ، عليهم تقوم الساعة . صحيح مسلم رقم ١٩٢٤

It is narrated from Hadrat 'Abdullâh bin 'Amr bin al 'Âs ﷺ... "then Allâh will send a breeze like a breeze of musk. Its touch will be like the touch of silk. It will not leave anybody in whose heart there is *îmân* equal to a seed except that it will take his (soul – [T]). The worst of people will remain. Upon them *Qiyâmah* will happen."[202]

[202] Sahîh Muslim, Hadîth 1924

THE MOST IMPORTANT TASKS OF HADRAT MAHDÎ ﷺ

1. He will fill the earth with justice and equity just as it was filled with oppression and tyranny. There will be no oppression in his actions and rule.

2. His justice and equity will be general, encompassing everyone, (i.e. without favouritism, nepotism etc. – [T])

3. He will establish a *khilâfah* upon the radiant ways of the *khilâfah ar râshida.*

4. Islâm will gain dominance in the earth in his time and Islâm will be established.

5. He will purify the hearts of the *ummah.*

6. He will make *ta'lîm* (teaching of *dîn*) widespread.

7. He will purify people from *shirk*[203] and *bid'ât.*[204]

Hadrat Gangohî رحمة الله عليه says,

فيزكيهم (أى المهدي) ويعلمهم ويطهرهم عـن دنـس البـدعات ويكملهـم .

الكوكب الدري ٢/٥٧

[203] Polytheism. – [T]
[204] Innovations in *dîn.* – [T]

He (Hadrat Mahdî ﷺ) will purify them, teach them and cleanse them from the filth of innovations and he will make them complete.[205]

8. *Dajjâl* will emerge in the seventh year after his (Hadrat Mahdî 's ﷺ - [T]) emergence and he will fight *Dajjâl* alongside Hadrat 'Îsâ الَعَلَيْهِ.

9. Wealth in his time will be so much like the heaps of grain in a mill.

والمال كداس . الفتن ٢٥٣ رقم ٩٩٢

And wealth will be in heaps.[206]

10. There will be livestock in abundance during his time.

11. Abundant beneficial rain will fall.

12. There will be many crops harvested.

عن أبي سعيد الخدري رضي الله عنه قال : قال رسول الله صلى الله عليه وسلم

: "يخرج في آخر أمتي المهدي ، يسقيه الله الغيث ، وتخرج الأرض نباتها ،

ويعطي المال صحاحا ، وتكثر الماشية ، وتعظم الامة — ويعيش سبعا أو ثمانيا

يعني حججا . مستدرك للحاكم ٤/٦٠١ رقم ٨٦٧٣

Hadrat Abû Sa'îd al Khudrî ﷺ says, Rasûlullâh ﷺ said, "*The Mahdî will emerge in the final era of my ummah. Allâh will send abundant*

---

[205] Al Kaukab Ad Durrî vol.2 p.57

[206] Al Fitan p.253, Hadîth 992

rain; the earth will bring forth its crops. He will distribute wealth properly. There will be many cattle and the ummah will have great honour at that time. He will live for seven or eight years."[207]

13. The conditions will be so good and prosperous that those who are living will wish that those who passed away were still alive and could see these prosperous conditions.

لا تدع السماء من قطرها شيئا الا صبته مدرارا ، ولا تدع الأرض من ماءها شيئا الا أخرجته ، حتى تتمنى الأحياء الأموات . مصنف عبد الرزاق ١١/٣٧٢ رقم ٢٠٧٧٠

The sky will not leave any of its drops; the earth will not leave any of its water except that it will bring it forth. This will be to such a degree that the living will desire that the dead be alive.[208]

14. He ﷺ will fill the hearts of people with contentment due to his generosity.

ويملأ قلوب امة محمد غنى . منتخب كنز العمال ٦/٢٩

He will fill the hearts of the *ummah* of Mu<u>h</u>ammad ﷺ with contentment.[209]

15. He will distribute wealth liberally.

---

[207] Mustadrak <u>H</u>âkim vol.4 p.601, <u>H</u>adîth 8673

[208] Mu<u>s</u>annaf ʿAbdur Razzâq vol.11 p.372, <u>H</u>adith 20770

[209] Muntakhab Kanz al ʿUmmâl vol.6 p.29

16. He will take out the treasure that is in front of the door of the *Ka'bah* and distribute it among the Muslims. The name of this treasure is *Ritâj al Ka'bah.*

Note: There is a narration about *Ritâj al Ka'bah* recorded in *Muntakhab Kanz ul 'Ummâl*. Muftî Nizâm ud Dîn Shâmzî رحمة الله عليه says that it is sahîh.[210]

حدثنا ابن وهب ، عن إسحق بن يحيى بن طلحة التميمي ، عن طاؤس قال : ودع عمر بن الخطاب رضي الله عنه البيت ثم قال : والله ما أراني أدع خزائن البيت وما فيه من السلاح والمال أم أقسمه في سبيل الله ؟ فقال له علي بن أبي طالب رضي الله عنه : امض يا أمير المؤمنين ! فلست بصاحبه ، إنما صاحبه منا شاب من قريش يقسمه في سبيل الله في آخر الزمان . الفتن ٢٨٤ رقم ١٠٦٢

It is narrated from Tâ'ûs رحمة الله عليه, he says that 'Umar bin al Khattâb رضي الله عنه bid farewell to the *Ka'bah*. He then said, "By Allâh, I do not know whether I should leave the treasures of the *Ka'bah*, its weapons and wealth, or whether I should distribute it in the way of Allâh. Hadrat 'Alî رضي الله عنه said, "Leave it, for you are not responsible to do it. The person who will do it is a youngster from us – the *Quraysh*. He will distribute it in the way of Allâh during the final era."[211]

---

[210] 'Aqîdah Zuhûr e Mahdî p.70, Sahîh is a narration whose narrators are just, remember completely, its chain is linked at every point and there is no cause for weakness in it. [Irshâd Usûl ul Hadîth p.60] – [T]

[211] Al Fitan p.284, Hadîth 1062

17. He will give wealth liberally without counting.[212]

18. The Muslim *ummah* will attain a high status in honour.

19. The prosperous conditions of his time and his proverbial generosity is recorded in the following narration,

عن أبي هريرة رضي الله عنه ، قال رسول الله صلى الله عليه وسلم : "أبـشروا بالمهدي رجل من قريش من عترتي ، يخرج في إخـتلاف مـن النـاس وزلـزال فيملأ الأرض قسطا وعدلا كما ملئت ظلـما وجـورا ويرضى سـاكن الأرض ويقسم المال صحاحا بالسوية ويملأ قلوب أمة محمد غنى ويسعهم عدله حتى أنه يأمر مناديا ينادي من له حاجة إلى ، فما يأتيه أحد إلا رجـل واحـد ، يأتيـه فيسئله فيقول : ائت السادن حتى يعطيك ، فيأتيه فيقول : أنا رسـول المهـدي إليك لتعطيني مالا ، فيقول : احث ، فيحثى ولا يـستطيع أن يحملـه ، فيلقـى حتى يكون قدر ما يستطيع أن يحمله ، فيخـرج بـه فينـدم فيقـول : أنـا كنـت أجشع امة محمد نفسا ، كلهم دعى إلى هذا المال فتركـه غـيري ، فـيرد عليـه ، فيقول : إنا لا نقبل شيئا أعطيناه ، فيلبث في ذلك ستا أو سبعا أو ثمانيا أو تسع سنين ، ولا خير في الحيوة بعده . منتخب كنز العمال ٦/٢٩

Hadrat Abû Hurayrah ⬥ narrates, Rasûlullâh ﷺ said,"Rejoice with the glad-tidings of the Mahdî, a person of Quraysh, of my family. He will emerge at the time of difference of opinion and earthquakes. He

---

[212] The wording in the original Urdu is proverbial. The literal translation is he will give wealth that fills both his hands, i.e. liberally. – [T]

will fill the earth with justice and equity just as it was filled with oppression and tyranny. All the inhabitants of the earth and heavens will be happy with him. He will distribute wealth correctly with justice. He will fill the hearts of the ummah of Mu<u>h</u>ammad with contentment and his equity will spread among them all. This will be to such a degree that he will tell his announcer to announce, "Does anyone have a need to place before me?" A single person will come to him. He ﷺ *will say, "Go to the treasurer, he will give you." That person will go to the treasurer and say that Mahdî has sent me so that you may give me some wealth. The treasurer will tell him to take it himself. That person will take more than he can carry. He will then put back until it reaches an amount that he will be able to carry. He will leave and become ashamed saying, "I am the greediest person in the ummah of Mu<u>h</u>ammad* ﷺ*. Everyone was called to this wealth and they left it, besides me." He will want to return that wealth. The treasurer will say that we do not take back what has been given. Mahdî will then live for six, seven, eight, or nine years. After that, there will be no good in staying alive.*[213]

SOCIAL LIFE DURING THE ERA OF THE *MAHDÎ*

A great favour of Allâh ﷻ upon this *ummah* during the time of <u>H</u>a<u>d</u>rat Mahdî ؓ will be that everyone will unanimously accept <u>H</u>a<u>d</u>rat Mahdî ؓ to be his or her leader and guide. There will not be any difference of opinion. It will be an example of great love and unity.

---

[213] Muntakhab Kanz ul 'Ummâl vol.6 p.29

عن دينار بن دينار قال : يظهر المهدي وقد تفرق الفئ فيواسى بين الناس في ما وصل إليه لا يوثر أحدا ، ويعمل بالحق حتى يموت ثم تصير الدنيا بعده هرج . الفتن ٢٥٤ رقم ٩٩٥

It is narrated from Dînâr bin Dînâr who said, "*Mahdî* will emerge when the people will be in disarray. He will console the people. He will not give preference to some over others. He will deal correctly until his demise. Then corruption and trouble will erupt in the entire world.[214]

IMPORTANT INCIDENTS

There are some very important incidents mentioned in the Ahâdîth. They will take place in the final era close to *Qiyâmah*. However, there is no clarity as to exactly when they will occur. All these incidents will occur at the time very close to the emergence of Hadrat Mahdî ﷺ. We come to this conclusion after pondering over the various narrations as well as the method in which they have been mentioned. (We understand this – [T]) also from studying the works of our pious predecessors about Hadrat Mahdî ﷺ. These incidents are recollected below:

(1) RESTRICTIONS UPON 'IRÂQ, EGYPT AND SYRIA FROM THE ROMANS AND NON-ARAB NATIONS

عن أبي نضرة قال : كنا عند جابر بن عبد الله فقال : يوشك أهل العراق أن لا يجئ إليهم قفيز ولا درهم ، قلنا من أين ذاك؟ قال من قبل العجم ، يمنعون

214 Al Fitan p.254, Hadîth 995

ذاك . ثم قال يوشك أهل الشام أن لا يجئ إليهم دينار ولا مدى ، قلنا من أين ذاك قال من قبل الروم ، ثم سكت هنية ، ثم قال : قـال رسـول الله صـلى الله عليه وسلم : يكون في آخر أمتي خليفة يحثى المال حثيا ولا يعـده عـدا ، قـال قلت لأبي نضرة وأبي العلاء : أتريان أنـه عمـر بـن عبـد العزيـز فقـالا : لا .

صحيح مسلم ٢/٣٩٥ رقم ٢٩١٣

<u>H</u>a<u>d</u>rat Abû Na<u>d</u>rah ﷺ says, "We were sitting by Jâbir bin 'Abdullâh ﷺ." He (Jâbir ﷺ) said, "Soon the condition of the people of 'Irâq will be such that not even a qafîz or a dirham will come to them." We said, "From whom (will these restrictions) come?" He said, "From the non-Arabs."

After a little while he said, "Soon the condition of the people of Shâm will be such that not even a dînâr or a mudd will come to them." We said, "From whom (will these restrictions) be?" He said, "From the Romans."

He remained silent for a while and then said, "Rasûlullâh ﷺ said, "There will be a khalîfah in the final era of my ummah who will distribute wealth liberally and he will not even count it." The narrator says, "I asked Abû Na<u>d</u>rah and Abul 'Alâ', "Do you think it is 'Umar bin 'Abdul 'Azîz?" They said, "No."

'Allâmah Taqî 'Uthmânî *dâmat barakâtuhu* writes in his *Takmila Fat<u>h</u> al Mulhim*, quoting *Qur<u>t</u>ubî*, that a group of *'ulemâ'* incline to the view that <u>H</u>a<u>d</u>rat Mahdî ﷺ is referred to in this narration. The text is presented hereunder,

وذهب جمع من العلماء إلى أن المراد منه خليفة الله المهدي الذي يخـرج في آخـر الزمان . تكمله فتح الملهم ٦/٣٢٩

(2) THE SUDDEN INCURSION OF THE ROMANS INTO SYRIA

We learn from some books that the Christians will be ruling Syria. Their rule will stretch until Khaybar.

(3) THE FEW ARABS DURING THAT ERA – THEY WILL GATHER AT A PLACE CLOSE TO *BAYT AL MUQADDAS*

يا رسول الله : فأين العرب يومئذ؟ قال : هم يومئذ قليل ببيت المقدس . ابن ماجة ٣٠٨ رقم ٤٠٧٧

Someone asked, "O messenger of Allâh, where will the Arabs be at that time?" Rasûlullâh ﷺ replied, "They will be few in Bayt al Muqaddas."[215]

(4) PEOPLE WILL LEAVE MADÎNAH DUE TO LACK OF DESIRE AND INCLINATION

People will leave Madînah Munawwarah due to lack of inclination. They will hear that the gardens and crops in a certain place are flourishing, so they will leave, whereas Madînah Munawwarah is better for them. Allâh ﷻ will let Madînah Munawwarah be inhabited by better people that were there.

عن جابر بن عبد الله رضي الله عنه – مرفوعا – لا يخرج رجل من المدينة رغبة عنها إلا أبدلها الله خير منه ، وليسمعن ناس برخص من أسعار وريف فيتبعونه ، والمدينة خير لهم لو كانوا يعلمون . مستدرك للحاكم ٤/٥٠١ رقم ٨٤٠

---

[215] Sunan Ibn Mâjah p.308, Hadîth 4077

In a marfû ʿ narration of H̲ad̲rat Jâbir bin ʿAbdullâh ﷺ it is stated that no one will leave Madînah except that Allâh will place others better than him, and those that hear of cheap prices and agricultural development will leave, whereas Madînah is better for them if they knew.[216]

(5) THE APPEARANCE OF A MOUNTAIN OF GOLD

Imâm Muslim رحمة الله عليه has recorded the following narration of H̲ad̲rat Ubayy bin Kaʿb ﷺ,

عن أبى بن كعب رضي الله عنه قال : إني سمعت رسول الله صلى الله عليه وسلم يقول : "يوشك الفرات أن يحسر عن جبل من ذهب ، فإذا سمع به الناس ساروا إليه ، فيقول من عنده : لئن تركنا الناس يأخذون منه ليذهبن به كله – قال : فيقتتلون عليه فيقتل من كل مائة تسعة وتسعون". صحيح مسلم ٢/٣٩١ رقم ٢٨٩٥

H̲ad̲rat Ubayy bin Ka'b ﷺ narrates, "I heard Rasûlullâh ﷺ saying, "Soon, a mountain of gold will appear from the Euphrates River. When people will hear of this, they will leave for there. The people who live there will say, "If we leave these people to take the gold, all will be taken." He ﷺ said, "They will fight over it. Ninety nine percent of the people will be killed (in this war – [T])."

A similar narration of H̲ad̲rat Thaubân ﷺ is recorded in *Sunan Ibn Mâjah,*

---

[216] Mustadrak H̲âkim vol.4 p.501, H̲adîth 840

عن ثوبان رضي الله عنه قال : قال رسول الله صلى الله عليه وسلم : "يقتتـل
عند كنزكم ثلاثة ، كلهم ابن خليفة ، ثم لا يصير الى واحد منهم ، ثـم تطلـع
الرايات السود من قبل المشرق — فيقتلونكم قتلا لم يقتله قوم ، ثم ذكر شيئا لا
أحفظه . فقال : فإذا رأيتموه فبايعوه ولـو حبـوا عـلى الـثلج فإنـه خليفـة الله
المهدي . سنن ابن ماجة ٣١٠

Hadrat Thaubân ﷠ narrates that *Rasûlullâh* ﷺ said, "*Three people
will fight over your treasure. All of them will be sons of khulafâ'. None
of them will get the treasure. A black flag will then appear from the
east. They will fight you so severly that no nation has fought you in
such a way before.*" *Hadrat Thaubân* ﷠ says, "*He* ﷺ *then said
something that I do not remember.*" *He* ﷺ *then said, "When you see
him, then pledge allegiance to him immediately, even if you have to
come crawling over ice. He is definitely the khalîfah of Allâh, the
Mahdî.*"[217]

Hâfiz Ibn *Hajar* 'Asqalânî ﵀ says in *Fath al Bârî*,
'If the treasure referred to in this *Hadîth* is the one that is
mentioned in the narration of the mountain of gold, then it is
proof that these incidents will occur at the time of the emergence
of *Mahdî*.'[218]

---

[217] Sunan Ibn Mâjah p.310
[218] Fath al Bârî vol.13 p.81

(6) KILLING OF THE PURE SELF

The crux of a narration of *Musannaf Ibn Abî Shaybah* is that Hadrat Mahdî ﵁ will emerge after the killing of a pure self, i.e. a great pious person.[219]

(7) UNITY OF THE MUSLIMS AND CHRISTIANS

This subject is discussed in the following narration of *Sunan Abû Dâwûd,*

عن الهدنة رضي الله عنه قال : سمعت رسول الله صلى الله عليه وسلم يقول : "ستصالحون الروم صلحا آمنا ، فتغزون أنتم وهم عدوا من ورائكم ، فتنصرون وتغنمون وتسلمون ثم ترجون حتى تنزلوا بمرج ذي تلول ، فيرفع رجل من أهل النصرانية الصليب فيقول : غلب الصليب – فيغضب رجل من المسلمين ، فيدقه – فعند ذلك تغدر الروم وتجمع للملحمة" . سنن أبو داؤد ٢/٥٩٠ رقم ٤٢٩٢

It is narrated from Hadrat Hudnah ﵁, "I heard Rasûlullâh ﷺ saying, "The Muslims and Romans will share a peaceful treaty. They will jointly fight an enemy that is behind you. They will be helped, will gain booty and will return safely to a lush hill. A Christian will raise the cross and say, "The cross has overpowered." A Muslim will be angered at this and will break it. The Christians will break the treaty and will prepare for a great war."[220]

---

[219] Musannaf Ibn Abî Shaybah vol.15 p.199, Hadîth 19499

[220] Sunan Abû Dâwûd vol.2 p.590, Hadîth 4292, this narration is also recorded in Sahîh Muslim, in brief.

(8) A BLOODY WAR DURING THE DAYS OF HAJJ

We learn from a narration that there will be a bloody war during the days of *Hajj* in the blessed land of Mina. It will be so severe that blood will be spilt on the *Jamarah al 'Aqabah*.

عن عمرو بن شعيب ، عن أبيه ، عن جده قال : قال رسول الله صلى الله عليه وسلم : في ذي القعدة تحازب القبائل ، وعامئذ ينهب الحاج فتكون ملحمة بمنى ، فيكثر فيه القتلى ، وتسفك فيها الدماء حتى تسيل دماؤهم على عقبة الجمرة – الخ . الفتن ٢٦٧ رقم ٩٩٤

Hadrat 'Amr bin Shu 'ayb narrates from his father who narrates from his grandfather ﷺ *that Rasûlullâh* ﷺ *said, "During Dhûl Qa 'dah, the tribes will be split into groups. There will be plundering amongst the Hujjâj that year and there will be a war in Mina. There will be many dead and blood will be spilt to such a degree that their blood will flow on the Jamarah al 'Aqabah."*[221]

(9) ANOTHER WAR

Study the following narration of *Mustadrak Hâkim* regarding another war,

أخبرني أحمد بن محمد بن سلمة العنزي ، حدثنا عثمان بن سعيد الدارمي ، حدثنا سعيد بن أبي مريم ، أنبأنا نافع بن يزيد ، حدثني عياش بن عباس أن الحارث بن يزيد حدثه أنه سمع عبد الله بن زرير الغافقي يقول سمعت علي بن أبي طالب رضي الله عنه يقول : ستكون فتنة يحصل الناس منها كما يحصل

221 Al Fitan p.267, Hadîth 994

الذهب في المعدن – فلا تسبوا أهل الشام ، وسبوا ظلمتهم – فإن فيهم الأبدال ، وسيرسل الله إليهم سيبا من السماء فيغرقهم حتى لو قاتلتهم الثعالب غلبتهم – ثم يبعث الله عند ذلك رجلا من عترة الرسول صلى الله عليه وسلم في اثنى عشر ألفا إن قلوا ، وخمسة عشر ألفا إن كثروا – أمارتهم أو علامتهم "أمت أمت" على ثلث رايات يقاتلهم أهل سبع رايات ، ليس من صاحب رأية إلا وهو يطمع بالملك ، فيقتتلون ويهزمون ثم يظهر الهاشمي فيرد الله إلى الناس الفتهم ونعمتهم – فيكونون على ذلك حتى يخرج الدجال – هذا حديث صحيح الإسناد ولم يخرجاه . مستدرك ٤/٥٩٦ رقم ٨٦٥٨

Hadrat 'Alî ؓ said, "Soon there will be fitnah. In this (fitnah – [T]), people will be selected like how gold is from a mine. Do not speak ill of the people of Shâm, speak ill of their oppressors, for among them (the people of Shâm – [T]) are abdâl. Allâh will send rains upon the people of Shâm, (such rains– [T]) that will drown them. They will become so weak due to this that if a fox has to fight with them, the fox will overpower them.

Allâh will send a Hâshimî, i.e. Mahdî, who is from the progeny of Rasûlullâh ﷺ. He will have an army of twelve thousand at the least and fifteen thousand at the most. Their sign will be the call 'amit, amit'. Their army will be under three flags. The army facing them will be under seven flags, every soldier of their's will desire leadership. They will fight and will be defeated. Allâh will then give the Hâshimî, i.e. Mahdî, victory. Allâh will then return their lost blessings unto them. The people will then live in good conditions until the emergence of Dajjâl.[222]

GENERALLY UNDERSTOOD SIGNS OF THE EMERGENCE OF THE *MAHDÎ*

There are verifiable and unverifiable signs of Hadrat Mahdî ﷺ mentioned in the source books. Some of them are so easily understood that even a simpleton will be able to point out Hadrat Mahdî ﷺ upon witnessing them. We explain only two signs here,

(1) THE RISING OF A SIGN TOGETHER WITH THE SUN

أخبرنا عبد الرزاق ، عن معمر ، عن ابن طاؤس ، عـن عـلي بـن عبـد الله بـن عباس قال : لا يخرج المهدي حتى تطلع مع الشمس آية . مصنف عبد الرزاق ١١/٣٧٣ رقم ٢٠٧٧٥

It is narrated from ʿAlî bin ʿAbdullâh bin ʿAbbâs ﷺ, "*Mahdî* will not emerge until a sign rises together with the sun."[223]

Hadrat Muftî Nizâm ud Dîn Shâmzî رحمة الله عليه says that this narration is reliable.[224]

We find another *hasan*[225] narration of *Al Fitan* - compiled by Nuʿaym bin Hammâd,

---

[222] Mustadrak vol.4 p.596, Hadîth 8658

[223] Musannaf ʿAbdur Razzâq vol.11 p.373, Hadîth 20775

[224] ʿAqîdah Zuhûr e Mahdî p.53

[225] *Hasan* is translated as 'good'. There are two types of *Hasan* in Hadîth terminology. (i) *Hasan Li Dhâtihî* – the narration that fulfills all the conditions of *Sahîh li Dhâtihî*, except that the recording of the narrator is not complete. This

حدثنا ابن المبارك وابن ثور وعبد الرزاق ، عن معمر ، عن طاؤس ، عن علي

بن عبد الله بن عباس رضي الله عنه قال : لا يخرج المهدي حتى تطلع الـشـمس

آية . الفتن ٢٦٠ رقم ٩٥٩

It is narrated from ʿAlî bin ʿAbdullâh bin ʿAbbâs 🕮, "*Mahdî* will not emerge until the sun does not rise as a sign."

(2) KHURÂSÂN AND THE BLACK FLAGS

There are many narrations about the appearance of black flags from Khurâsân in the incidents at the time of the emergence of Hadrat Mahdî 🕮. A few of them are presented here with a basic analysis of their reliability,

عن علي ابن أبي طالب رضي الله عنه قال : إذا خرج خيل السفياني إلى الكوفـة

بعث في طلب أهل خراسان ، ويخرج أهل خراسان في طلب المهدي ، فيلتقـى

هو والهاشمي بـرايات سود ، على مقدمته شـعيب بـن صالح — فيلتقـى هـو

وأصحاب السفياني بباب اصطخر ، فتكون بيـنهم ملحمـة عظيمـة ، فتظهـر

الرايات السود وتهرب خيـل الـسفياني ، فعنـد ذلك يتمنى النـاس المهدي

ويطلبونه . منتخب كنز العمال على هامش مسند أحمد ٦/٣٣ والفتـن ٢١٨

رقم ٨٦٨

---

shortcoming cannot be made up by the same narration being narrated through other chains. (ii) *Hasan li Ghayrihî* – that narration in whose narrators all or some of the conditions of reliability are not found. However, this shortcoming can be made up if the narration is narrated through other chains. [Irshâd Uṣûl ul Hadîth pp.65-66] – [T]

(1) It is narrated from H̲ad̲rat ʿAlî ﷺ,[226] "When the army of *Sufyânî* will come out to Kûfah, he will then send an army in search of the people of Khurâsân. The people of Khurâsân will leave in search of the *Mahdî*. They (the people of Khurâsân – [T]) will meet them (the army of *Sufyânî* – [T]) and the *Hâshimî* with black flags. Shuʿayb bin S̲âli̲h will be at the head of this army. There will be a great battle between these two armies. The *Hâshimî* army will win and the army of *Sufyânî* will flee. The people will then hope for the *Mahdî* and will search for him."

Although this narration is classified as *mauqûf*[227], it will be placed in the category of marfûʿ (see footnote 53). This is because these very same words are found in *marfû*ʿ (see footnote 53) narrations. There is a well-known principle according to the scholars of H̲adîth and scholars of the principles of H̲adîth that the saying of a s̲ah̲âbî ﷺ that is beyond analogy will be placed in the category of *marfû*ʿ (see footnote 53).

عن ام سلمة رضي الله عنها إذا رأيتم الرايات السود قد جاءت من قبل خراسان فأتوها ، فإن فيها خليفة الله المهدي . منتخب كنز العمال ٦/٢٩

(2) It is narrated from H̲ad̲rat Umm e Salamah *rad̲iyallâhu anha*, "When you see black flags coming from Khurâsân, then go there because the *khalîfah* of Allâh, the *Mahdî*, is among them."[228]

This narration is reliable.[229]

---

[226] This narration is not translated word for word

[227] *Mauqûf* refers to a statement or action of a s̲ah̲âbî. [Irshâd Us̲ûl ul H̲adîth p.55] – [T]

[228] Muntakhab Kanz ul ʿUmmâl vol.6 p.29

[229] ʿAqîdah Z̲uhûr e Mahdî p.65

حدثنا محمد بن يحيى وأحمد بن يوسف ، قالا حدثنا عبد الرزاق ، عن سفيان الثوري ، عن خالد الحذاء ، عن أبي القلابة ، عن أبي أسماء الرحبى ، عن ثوبان رضي الله عنه قال : قال رسول الله صلى الله عليه وسلم : "يقتتل عند كنزكم ثلاثة ، كلهم ابن خليفة – ثم لا يصير إلى واحد منهم ، ثم تطلع الرايات السود من قبل المشرق – فيقتلونكم قتلا لم يقتله قوم – ثم ذكر شيئا لا أحفظه ، فقال : فإذا رأيتموه فبايعوه ولو حبوا على الثلج ، فإنه خليفة الله المهدي" .

سنن ابن ماجة ٣١٠

(3) *Hadrat Thaubân ﷺ narrates that Rasûlullâh ﷺ said, "Three people will fight over your treasure. All of them are sons of khulafâ' (princes). However, none of them will get it. Then, black flags will appear from the east. They will fight you in such a way that no nation has fought you before – the narrator says that he ﷺ said something which I do not remember – he ﷺ then said that when you see him, then pledge allegiance to him even if you have to go to him crawling on ice for he is the khalîfah of Allâh, the Mahdî."*[230]

This narration is also reliable although it is recorded in *Sunan Ibn Mâjah*. It is not from the *da'îf* (see footnote 83) and *maudû'* (see footnote 85) narrations of *Sunan Ibn Mâjah*. In addition, there are narrations of *Sunan Abû Dawûd* and *Mustadrak Hâkim* that corroborate this one. The narrations of other sahâbah ﷺ also support this one. For details, see *'Aqîdah Zuhûr e Mahdî* of Muftî Nizâm ud Dîn Shâmzî رحمة الله عليه pp.37-38.

---

[230] Sunan Ibn Mâjah p.310

ʿAllâmah Sindhî رحمۃ اللہ علیہ says, 'Abul H̲asan bin Sufyân رحمۃ اللہ علیہ has recorded this narration in his *Musnad* and Abû Nuʿaym has mentioned it in *Kitâb al Mahdî* from the chain of Ibrâhîm bin Suwayd Shâmî رحمۃ اللہ علیہ. This narration is s̲ah̲îh̲ (see footnote 210) through this chain and all the narrators are reliable.[231]

عن ثوبان رضي الله عنه قال : قال رسول الله صلى الله عليه وسلم إذا رأيتم الرايات السود قد جاءت من قبل خراسان فأتوها ، فإن فيها خليفة الله المهدي . رواه أحمد ٥/١٧٧ رقم ٢٢٧٤٦

(4) *It is narrated from H̲ad̲rat Thaubân ﷺ that Rasûlullâh ﷺ said, "When you see black flags coming from Khurâsân, then go there for among them is the khalîfah of Allâh, the Mahdî."*[232]

There is another narration of *Sunan Abû Dâwûd* regarding this in which it is explained that a king of Khurâsân will help H̲ad̲rat Mahdî ﷺ, it is quoted below,

عن هلال بن عمرو قال : سمعت عليا كرم الله وجهه يقول : قال النبي صلى الله عليه وسلم : "يخرج رجل من وراء النهر يقال له الحارث (بن في نسخة) حراث على مقدمته رجل يقال له منصور يؤطى أو يمكن لآل محمد كما مكنت قريش لرسول الله صلى الله عليه وسلم وجب على كل مؤمن نصره أو قال اجابته . أبو داؤد ٢/٥٨٩ رقم ٤٢٩٠

---

[231] Tarjumân us Sunnah vol.4 p.390
[232] Ah̲mad vol.5 p.177, H̲adîth 22746

(5) *It is narrated from Hilâl bin 'Amr, he says, "I heard 'Alî karramallâhu wajhahu saying, "Rasûlullâh ﷺ said, "A person will emerge from the land behind the river. His name will be Al Hârith (son of, in one copy) Harrâth. At the head (of this group – [T]) will be a man called Mansûr. He will give protection to the family of Muhammad (ﷺ - [T]) like the Quraysh gave to Rasûlullâh ﷺ. It is wâjib upon every believer to help him, or he said, (it is wâjib upon every believer to accept his command – [T])."*[233]

Shâh Rafi' ud Dîn writes in *'Alâmât e Qiyâmat* p.11, 'When the news of the emergence of *Mahdî* will spread throughout the Muslim world, then a person from Khurâsân will come to help him. At the front of this huge army will be a person called Mansûr. He will wipe out many Christians and atheists that they will find on the way."

Note: There is some debate on the authenticity of the above-mentioned narrations. However, strength is added to them considering that they are narrated through various chains.

SCRUTINY OF FAMOUS SIGNS AND THEIR REJECTION

(1) A SOLAR AND LUNAR ECLIPSE IN RAMADÂN BEFORE THE EMERGENCE OF THE *MAHDÎ*

A solar and lunar eclipse in the month of Ramadân before the emergence of Hadrat Mahdî عليه السلام is among the famous aspects regarding his (Hadrat Mahdî عليه السلام's) emergence. Such an amazing thing would have never happened since the creation of the heavens and the earth. Hadrat Shâh Rafi' ud Dîn رحمة الله عليه writes,

---

233 Sunan Abû Dâwûd vol.2 p.589, Hadîth 4290

'This has become famous on the basis of the following narration,

حدثنا أبو سعيد الاصطخري ، حدثنا محمد بن عبد الله بن نوفل ، حدثنا عبيد بن يعيش ، حدثنا يونس بن بكير ، عن عمرو بن شمر ، عن جابر ، عن محمد بن على قال : إن لمهدينا آيتين لم تكونا منذ خلق السموات والأرض ، ينكسف القمر لأول ليلة من رمضان وتنكسف الشمس في النصف منه ، ولم تكونا منذ خلق الله السموات والأرض . سنن الدار قطني ٢/٤٥ رقم ١٧٧٧ أو ١/١٨٨

It is narrated from Mu<u>h</u>ammad bin ʿAlî ﷺ, " Indeed for our *Mahdî* there are two signs that have never happened since the creation of the heavens and the earth. (The first is that) there will be a lunar eclipse on the first night of Rama<u>d</u>ân. (The second is that) there will be a solar eclipse halfway through the same Rama<u>d</u>ân. These two signs would never have occurred since the creation of the heavens and the earth."

The first thing that one should remember concerning this narration is that this narration is definitely not a <u>H</u>adîth. It is a statement of Mu<u>h</u>ammad bin ʿAlî رحمة الله عليه. It is a false allegation to classify this as a statement of Rasûlullâh ﷺ until clear proof does not show otherwise. In fact, it will necessitate the following <u>H</u>adîth,

من كذب على متعمدا الخ

"He who willfully attributes a false statement to me should build his abode in the fire."

The chain of narration of this statement of Mu<u>h</u>ammad bin ʿAlî is rejected on the following premises,

- One narrator of this statement is ʿAmr bin Shamr. Hâfiz Ibn Hajar ʿAsqalânî رحمة الله عليه and ʿAllâmah Shams ud Dîn Dhahabî رحمة الله عليه have used harsh words for him, like, *kadh dhâb*[234], *râfidî*, a swearer of the sahâbah ﷺ, *matrûk al hadîth* etc. One of his very bad habits was that he used to attribute fabricated narrations to reliable narrators and narrate them. For this reason, these scholars have passed the decision not to accept his narrations.[235]

  ʿAmr bin Shamr used to narrate *maudû*ʿ (see footnote 85) narrations from Jâbir Juʿfî.
- The second narrator of this statement is Jâbir Juʿfî. He is very greatly debated (*mutakallam fîh*). He was a staunch shîʿa and a swearer of the sahâbah ﷺ. Imâm Muslim رحمة الله عليه has explained the *jarh* (see footnote 193) of Jâbir Juʿfî done by four great scholars through six chains on p.15 of his introduction to *Sahîh Muslim*. His belief in *irjâ*ʿ[236] is at the top of the list. Imâm Abû Hanîfah رحمة الله عليه says, "From all the liars that I have come across, I have never seen a greater liar than Jâbir Juʿfî. Details of Jâbir Juʿfî are explained in *Tahdhîb ut Tahdhîb* vol.1 p.352.
- The third narrator is Muhammad bin ʿAlî. Many narrators have this name. There is no clarity about who this Muhammad bin ʿAlî is. Therefore, this narrator is also *majhûl* (see footnote 77). To take Muhammad bin ʿAlî to mean Hadrat Bâqir رحمة الله عليه, as is the opinion of some scholars is also without proof.

---

234 A great liar – [T]

235 Lisân ul Mîzân vol.4 p.422, Mîzân al Iʿtidâl vol.2 p.262

236 Being part of the Murjiʿa sect – [T]

This narration has no credibility in ,the light of the above-mentioned reasons. It cannot be presented as proof for such an important subject like the emergence of Mahdî. Similarly, this sign of an eclipse at the time of Hadrat Mahdî cannot be proven from this narration.

A similar narration is found in *'Iqd ud Durar fî Akhbâr al Muntazar* of Shaykh Yûsuf Maqdisî and in the shî'a book, *'Bashâratul Anâm bi Zuhûr al Mahdî 'alayhî as Salâm lil Kâzimî'*. This narration states, 'The solar eclipse will take place halfway through Ramadân and the lunar eclipse will take place at the end of Ramadân. These two signs would have never happened since Hadrat Âdam came down to the earth.'

The discussion and debate on this narration is very similar to the discussion and debate on the narration of *Sunan Ad Dâr Qutnî* that was previously mentioned. Therefore, this narration is also not credible.[237]

Over and above this, from 1801 to 1900 there has been a solar and lunar eclipse in Ramadân five times. One aspect that also deserves attention is that from 1851 to 1895, in just 45 years, this (a solar and lunar eclipse) has occurred 3 times in Ramadân. One can judge from this as to how many times it would have occurred before that. Therefore, how can it be correct to say that this phenomenon would have never happened since the time that Allâh created the earth and skies? From this, we learn that this narration is not correct even from a factual point of view.[238]

---

[237] Adapted from Radd e Qâdiyâniyyat ke Zarî Usûl and Fiqhî Jawâhir p.3

[238] See Radd e Qâdiyâniyyat ke Zarî Usûl and Fiqhî Jawâhir for details

(2) WILL THERE BE A CALL FROM THE HEAVENS UPON THE EMERGENCE OF HADRAT MAHDÎ ؓ?

One of the signs of the emergence of Hadrat Mahdî ؓ explained in the Urdu and Arabic books written on the subject of Hadrat Mahdî ؓ is that when Hadrat Mahdî ؓ emerges, there will be the following call from the skies,

هذا خليفة الله المهدي فأطيعوه

'This is the *khalîfah* of Allâh, the *Mahdî,* so obey him.'

This has also become famous among the people. Therefore, it is necessary for us to learn of its credibility.

Some of the narrations found in the different books of Hadîth are presented below,

حدثنا ابراهيم بن محمد بن عرق الحمصي ، حدثنا عبد الوهاب بن ضحاك ، حدثنا اسمعيل بن عياش ، عن صفوان بن عمرو ، عن عبد الرحمن بن جبير بن نفير ، عن كثير بن مرة ، عن عبد الله بن عمرو بن العاص ، عن النبي صلى الله عليه وسلم أنه قال : يخرج المهدي زعلى رأسه ملك ينادي "إن هذا المهدي فاتبعوه" . مسند الشاميين ٢/٧١ رقم ٩٣٧

It is narrated from Hadrat ʿAbdullâh bin ʿAmr bin al ʿÂs ؓ that Rasûlullâh ﷺ said, "The Mahdî will emerge in such a way that there will be an angel above his head calling out, 'This is the Mahdî, so follow him.'"[239]

Similarly, Imâm Ibn ʿAdî رحمة الله عليه has transmitted the following Hadîth in his *'Al Kâmil fi Duʿafâ ar Rijâl'* with its chains and texts with slight differences (among them – [T]).

---

[239] Musnad Ash Shâmiyyîn vol.2 p.71, Hadîth 937

حدثنا محمد بن عبيد الله بن فضيل ، حدثنا عبد الوهاب بن ضحاك ، حدثنا اسمعيل بن عياش ، عن صفوان بن عمرو ، عن عبد الرحمن بن جبير بن نفير ، عن كثير بن مرة ، عن عبد الله بن عمرو بن العاص ، عن النبي صلى الله عليه وسلم قال : "يخرج المهدي زعلى رأسه غمامة ، فيها مناد ينادي : ألا إن هذا المهدي فاتبعوه" . الكامل ٥١٥،٥١٦/٦

It is narrated from H̲ad̲rat ʿAbdullâh bin ʿAmr bin al ʿÂs ﷺ that Rasûlullâh ﷺ said, "The Mahdî will emerge in such a way that there will be a cloud above his head in which there will be an angel calling out, 'Indeed this is the Mahdî, so follow him.'"[240]

Both of these narrations are based on ʿAbdul Wahhâb bin D̲ah̲h̲âk bin Abân As Sulamî Al ʿUrd̲î. The imams of *Jarh̲ and Taʿdîl*[241] have mentioned very harsh statements regarding him. H̲âfiz̲ Ibn H̲ajar ʿAsqalânî رحمة الله عليه writes,

قال البخاري : عنده عجائب ، وقال أبو داؤد : كان يضع الحديث قد رأيته ، قال النسائ : ليس بثقة متروك ، وقال العقيلي والدار قطني والبيهقي : متروك . قال صالح بن محمد الحافظ : منكر الحديث ، عامة حديثه كذب . تهذيب التهذيب ٥٢٧،٥٢٨/٣

---

[240] Al Kâmil vol.6 pp.515-516

[241] *Jarh̲ and Taʿdîl* refers to the branch of H̲adîth study that deals with the reliability of narrators regarding certain words and the grading of those words. [Irshâd Us̲ûl ul H̲adîth p.150] – [T]

Bukhârî says, "He has strange narrations." Abû Dâwûd says, "I have seen him fabricate narrations." Nasâ'î says, "He is not *thiqah*[242] and is *matrûk*." ʿUqaylî, Ad Dâr Qutnî and Bayhaqî say, "He is *matrûk*." S̲âlih̲ bin Muh̲ammad al H̲âfiz̲ says, "He is *munkar al h̲adîth* (see footnote 76) and most of his Ah̲âdîth are lies."[243]

Statements of a similar nature is also mentioned in *Mîzân al I ʿtidâl* vol.2 pp.160-161.

Nuʿaym bin H̲ammâd ﷀ has also transmitted a few narrations on this subject in *Al Fitan*. However, they are *Âthâr* (see footnote 2) of the s̲ah̲âbah ﷜ and tâbiʿîn. Only one narration is *marfû* ʿ(see footnote 53) According to critical analysis, all these narrations are debated.

There are narrations of *Kanz ul ʿUmmâl* vol.14 p.584 and *Mus̲annaf Ibn Abî Shaybah* vol.7 p.531 that show the same meaning.

The summary of this study is that this narration cannot be used as proof for such an important subject like the emergence of *Mahdî* when looking at its chain of transmission.

UNTRACEABLE ASPECTS

Many things related to H̲ad̲rat Mahdî ﵀ have been mentioned. We tried throughout this book to present all that which is in line with authentic Ah̲âdîth. However, there are some things for which I could not find a narration backed by a strong chain, or some things are such that they are mentioned in the works of our

---

242 Reliable – [T]

243 Tahdhîb ut Tahdhîb vol.3 pp.527-528

luminaries but I could not find any reliable sources for them. Therefore, they are mentioned here separately.

1. Hadrat Mahdî ﵇ will misinform others and run from Makkah Mukarramah to Madînah Munawwarah.

2.

عن علي رضي الله عنه قال : يبعث جيش إلى المدينة فيأخذون من قدروا عليه من آل محمد صلى الله عليه وسلم ويقتل من بني هاشم رجالا ونساء ، فعند ذلك يهرب المهدي والمبيض من المدينة إلى مكة الخ . منتخب كنز العمال ٦/٣٣

It is narrated from Hadrat ʿAlî ﵁, "An army will be sent from Madînah. They will catch whoever they find belonging to the family of Muhammad ﷺ and they will kill many men and women from the *Banû Hâshim*. At that time, the *Mahdî* and *Mubayyid* will flee Madînah for Makkah."[244]

3. Hadrat Mahdî ﵇ will come out in this way that there will be a cloud above his head shading him. A hand will be protruding from this cloud and will be pointing towards Hadrat Mahdî ﵇.

4. The following call will be made from the heavens,

ألا ان الحق في آل محمد صلى الله عليه وسلم

Listen, the truth lies in the family of Muhammad ﷺ

---

[244] Muntakhab Kanz ul ʿUmmâl vol.6 p.33

5. The emergence of Hadrat Mahdî will take place after *'Ishâ' salâh* on the tenth of Muharram.

6. The clothing, sword and flag of Rasûlullâh will be with Hadrat Mahdî and the following words will be written on them,

البيعة لله

7. The sign of Rasûlullâh will be upon his shoulders.

8. The sea will split for Hadrat Mahdî just as it did for the *Banî Isrâ'îl.*

9. Hadrat Mahdî will place a dry branch in the earth and it will immediately become green and lush.

10. He will be given *'ilm e ladunnî*[245].

11. He (Hadrat Mahdî) will have a box. Most of the Jews will accept Islâm upon seeing it.

12. Hadrat Mahdî will have a stutter. Due to this, he will have difficulty in speaking and he will hit his thigh with his right hand.

There are many other things written on this subject that one will find and read but they have been left out because no

[245] Knowledge from Allâh , acquired without learning – [T]

authentic chain of transmission could be found for them. They were also left out for brevity.

Narrations stating the above-mentioned things are either *da'îf* (see footnote 83) or *maqtû'* (see footnote 61). Some are also *maudû'*(see footnote 85). These things have become famous among people. That is why we have explained them here to inform them (of its unreliability – [T]).

KASHF AND ILHÂM AND THEIR STATUS IN THE *SHARÎ'AH*

There are many *mukâshafât*[246] regarding Hadrat Mahdî ﷺ that are narrated from the luminaries. Many books mention these *mukâshafât* with great importance. Some people narrate these *mukâshafât* with no caution whatsoever. They then gradually become famous among the people and then the people take it to be based on reliable sources.

There are some *mukâshafât,* prophesies and sayings of luminaries of the recent past that are narrated. Leaving aside whether it is correct or not to attribute them to these luminaries of *dîn,* we only intend to explain the reality and status of *kashf* and *ilhâm.*

The lexical meaning of *kashf* is 'to open'. The technical definition of *kashf* is 'the knowledge that Allâh ﷻ opens to somebody, whether it be a *nabî* or *walî*[247], obedient or sinner, Muslim or non-Muslim, man or animal.' The implication of *kashf*

---

[246] Disclosures – [T]
[247] A very pious servant of Allâh ﷻ - [T]

is general. However, according to our common usage, *kashf* is also special with the pious as *ilhâm* is.

Although *kashf* and *ilhâm* differ in their comprehended meanings, and they are similar in implication, they are both *zannî*[248] in the light of *sharî'ah.*[249] It is not *wâjib* or desired to have *îmân* in them. *Kashf* and *ilhâm* are neither part of the integrals of Islâm nor are they part of the principles of *dîn* nor do they stand as proof of *sharî'ah*. The only thing that we can do is make a premature surmise of it that could or could not turn out to be reality. It is similar to the interpretation of dreams.

A similar discussion is found in *Khayr al Fatâwâ* of Maulânâ Khayr Muhammad Jâlandharî رحمة الله عليه [vol.1 pp.67-68]. It was written in reply to a request for a *fatwâ*.

Hadrat Maulânâ Muhammad Yûsuf Ludhiyânwî رحمة الله عليه has written the following in reply to a question regarding this,

'The meaning of *kashf* is the disclosure of something. *Ilhâm* refers to something that is put in the heart and the meaning of *bashârat* is glad-tidings, like seeing a good dream.'

He further writes,

'*Kashf, ilhâm* and *bashârat* is possible after the demise of Rasûlullâh ﷺ, but it is not a proof of *sharî'ah*. Claims that it is indisputable cannot be made and no-one can claim that it must be believed.'

He writes in reply to another question,

'A person who is not a *nabî* can get *kashf* or *ilhâm* but it is not a proof. A ruling cannot be based on it. It will be judged in the light of *sharî'ah*. If it is correct, it will be accepted, otherwise not. This

---

248 *Zannî* refers to anything that is of a grading other than *Mutawâtir* – [T]
249 Disputable

will be the case when the person follows the *sunnah* of Rasûlullâh ﷺ and is an adherent of the *sharî 'ah*. If a person lives against the *sunnah* of Rasûlullâh ﷺ, then his claim of *kashf* and *ilhâm* is a devilish plot.'[250]

Kashf and *ilhâm* is not a proof in *dîn* and religion. The meaning of this is that the phenomenon of *kashf* is proven from authentic texts but there is possibility of error with regards to the specific time and place in the *kashf* of people other than the *Ambiyâ'*. Hadrat Maulânâ Rashîd Ahmad Gangohî رحمة الله عليه says,

'There are three types of *mukâshafât*. One is subject to divine working. Muslims and non-Muslims are on par in this type. One type is from the *lauh e mahfûz*[251]. This is special with Muslims. However, the following verse (clarifies its reality – [T]),

يَمْحُو اللهُ مَا يَشَاء وَيُثْبِتُ وَعِندَهُ أُمُّ الْكِتَابِ

Allâh erases whatever He wills and keeps in place. With Him is the Mother of Books. [Sûrah ar Ra 'd (Thunder) 13:39]

One type is from the special knowledge of Allâh ﷻ. This is only for the *ambiyâ'*. There is possibility of error in the first two, but not in the third. This is because specification of place and time is by estimation, but the past, present and future are all the same in the knowledge of Allâh ﷻ. Therefore, the knowledge of the *ambiyâ'* is pure from error.[252]

---

[250] Âp ke Masâ'il Aur un ka Hal vol.1 pp.34-35
[251] The protected tablet – [T]
[252] Arwâh e Thalâtha p.295

There has been *mukâshafât* of certain scholars about the specific year in which H̲ad̲rat Mahdî ﷺ will emerge. However, they were proven wrong. H̲ad̲rat Maulânâ Muh̲ammad Yaʿqûb Nânotwî رحمة الله عليه writes in one of his letters[253],

'Some people of *kashf* think that the emergence of Mah̲dî and other promised signs of *Qiyâmah* will take place in the next century. Some have said that this time is still far away. Allâh knows best. It is unnecessary to state anything with regard to that which has been written after that. Whatever Allâh wants, that will happen.'[254]

He رحمة الله عليه writes in another letter[255] in the interpretation of a dream,

'What is surprising about meeting Imâm Mahdî? One could attain it because many signs have become apparent. What is surprising if his emergence takes place in the first or second year of this century, in accordance to the *kashf* of the pious?' Allâh knows best.[256]

We learn from the above that some people of *kashf* had *kashf* of the emergence of H̲ad̲rat Mahdî ﷺ in 1301 or 1302. We are now in 1426[257] and H̲ad̲rat Mahdî ﷺ has not yet emerged.

The *kashf* of the friends of Allâh will be considered when it is not in conflict with the Qur'ân, H̲adîth, *Ijmâʿ* and correct *Qiyâs.* This is agreed upon by the former and latter day scholars as explained by Qâd̲î Thanâ' ullâh Pânîpattî رحمة الله عليه in *'Irshâd ut*

---

253 Sent on 12 Shawwâl 1294

254 Maktûbât wa Bayâd̲ e Yaʿqûbî p.111

255 Sent on 24 Dhû al Qaʿdah 1299

256 Ibid p.129

257 This is the year when the original Urdu book was written. This translation is being prepared in 1431. – [T]

Tâlibîn'. To specify a year for the emergence of Hadrat Mahdî ﷺ is in conflict with the authentic *nusûs*[258]. The demand of the *nusûs* is that the emergence of Hadrat Mahdî ﷺ is kept hidden by Allâh ﷻ. The time will come when this secret will be suddenly opened. This matter has been kept so secret that Hadrat Mahdî ﷺ will not be aware of his own position just before his emergence.[259]

The difference between *wahî, ilhâm* and *kashf* can be understood in the following way,

Wahî refers to only that knowledge which is placed in the heart of a *nabî*. It matters not in which way it happens. The scholars of Hadîth have explained different types of *wahî*. Anyway, the knowledge of *wahî* is indisputable and it is necessary to believe in it.

Ilhâm is that knowledge which is placed in a blessed heart that has a proper nature. This is without striving for it and deducing it. If the placing of this knowledge is in the heart of a *nabî*, then it is called *wahî* and it will be indisputable. If it is placed in the heart of anyone else, then it will called *ilhâm* according to common usage. This knowledge is *zannî* (see footnote 248).

Another difference between *wahî* and *ilhâm* is that the *wahî* and *ilhâm* of the *ambiyâ'* consists of commands and prohibitions. Therefore, it is *wâjib* for the *nabî* to propagate it. The *ilhâm* of the pious consists of glad-tidings and deep understanding. It is not *wâjib* upon them to propagate their *ilhâm*. It is better for them to keep it hidden until a *shar'î* or *dînî* need arises.

---

[258] Clear texts of the Qur'ân and Hadîth – [T]

[259] Adapted from Fiqhî Jawâhir vol.3 pp.84-85

Hadrat Muftî Maḥmûd Hasan Gangohî رحمةالله once narrated an incident,
'Twenty five years ago, one person told me that Imâm Mahdî was born from such a time. Hadrat Mîkâ'îl عليه السلام has informed me. He has not emerged yet. He indicated a cubit's length saying that it is equal to a cubit's length.'[260]

THE COMPANIONS OF HADRAT MAHDÎ ؏

There are many signs and glad-tidings in the narrations regarding those fortunate Muslims who will get the opportunity to strive for universal îmânî revival together with Hadrat Mahdî ؏.

1. His companions will be beloved to Allâh ﷻ and Allâh ﷻ will forgive them.

2. Their hearts will be united.

3. They will fear none but Allâh ﷻ.

4. The companions of Hadrat Mahdî ؏ will initially be weak as far as apparent strength is concerned.

5. The 313 people that will pledge allegiance at his hands first, will be the highest in îmânî status after the khayr al qurûn (see footnote 145).

---

[260] Malfuẓât Faqîh ul Ummah vol.9 p.55

6. The companions of H̲ad̲rat Mahdî ﷺ together with H̲ad̲rat ʿÎsâ ﷺ will afterwards fight against the Jews in the final battle.

7. One division of the troops of the companions of H̲ad̲rat Mahdî ﷺ will fight against *Dajjâl.*

8. The *kaʿbah* will be their place of safety.

9. They will not be scared of anyone nor will they see somebody and become pleased. They will be involved in their pursuit. Their goal (to elevate the word of Allâh ﷻ) will be of top priority. They will also be united.

حدثنا أبو العباس محمد بن يعقوب ، حدثنا الحسن بن علي بن عفان العامري ، حدثنا عمرو بن محمد العنقري ، حدثنا يونس بن أبي اسحق ، أخبرني عمار الذهبي ، عن أبي الطفيل ، عن محمد بن الحنفية قال : كنا عند علي رضي الله عنه فسأله رجل عن المهدي فقال علي رضي الله عنه : هيهات ، ثم عقد بيده سبعا فقال ذاك يخرج في آخر الزمان ، إذا قال الرجل : الله الله : قتل فيجمع الله تعالى قوما قزع كقزع السحاب يؤلف الله بين قلوبهم ، لا يستوحشون إلى أحد ولا يفرحون بأحد يدخل فيهم ، على عدة أصحاب بدر ، لم يسبقهم الأولون ولا يدركهم الآخرون ، وعلى عدة أصحاب طالوت الذين جاوزوا معه النهر . هذا حديث صحيح على شرط الشيخين ، ولم يخرجاه . مستدرك للحاكم ٤/٥٥٤

It is narrated from Mu<u>h</u>ammad bin al H̲anafiyyah, "We were by ʿAlî ﷺ. One person asked him about the *Mahdî*. ʿAlî ﷺ said,

"Listen," He then made the sign of seven with his hands. He then said, "He will emerge in the final era in such conditions that if someone has to say, 'Allâh, Allâh', he will be killed. Allâh will then gather such a nation that will be like clouds. All joined to one another. Allâh will join their hearts. They will not be scared by anyone nor will they become happy at the one who joins them. They will be equal in number to those who fought at Badr. No one in the past will be able to surpass them in rank (except those of the *khayr al qurûn* (see footnote 145)), nor will anyone in the future catch up to them. They will be the same in number as the companions of Ṯâlût who crossed the river with him."[261]

SPECIAL DISCUSSIONS CONCERNING THE COMPANIONS OF ḤAḌRAT MAHDÎ ⬥ IN THE AHÂDÎTH

1. The army that Ḥaḍrat Mahdî ⬥ will take from Madînah Munawwarah to Shâm will consist of the most virtuous Muslims of the world at that time. The following is mentioned in *Sahîh Muslim*,

فيخرج إليهم جيش من المدينة من خيار أهل الأرض يومئذ الخ . صحيح مسلم ٢/٣٩١ رقم ٢٨٩٧

2. The martyrs in Shâm will be the most virtuous martyrs after those of the era of Rasûlullâh ﷺ. The next part of the above-mentioned narration of *Sahîh Muslim* states,

---

[261] Mustadrak Ḥâkim vol.4 p.554

أفضل الشهداء عند الله . صحيح مسلم ٢/٣٩٢

3. Those Muslims who flee the battlefields of Shâm[262] due to the small number of Muslims and huge number of Christians will never be forgiven by Allâh ﷻ.

4. It is explained in the Hadîth that the leader of the army at the time of the conquest of Constantinople will be very good, i.e. Hadrat Mahdî رضي الله عنه. That army will also be very blessed.

5. After the conquest of Constantinople, the lies of *Dajjâl* will spread. Hadrat Mahdî رضي الله عنه will sent a contingent of ten men in order to establish the truth regarding *Dajjâl*. They will be the best people on the face of the earth at that time.

ANSWER TO AN IMPORTANT QUESTION

Will there be modern scientific inventions during the time of Hadrat Mahdî رضي الله عنه, or will it be like former times?

Many Muslims are confused over whether the world will return to previous ways or will modern scientific technology be present during (and after – [T]) the emergence of Hadrat Mahdî رضي الله عنه.

Regarding this subject, (we quote – [T]) an answer written by Hadrat Maulânâ Muhammad Yûsuf Ludhiyânwî رحمة الله عليه. (The following important question was posed to him – [T])

---

262 One third of the army

Question:

I read your article *'ʿAlâmât e Qiyâmat'* in the daily *'Jang'*[263]. There is no doubt that the solution to every query is satisfactory and they are backed by references from the Qur'ân and H̲adîth. This article also shows your knowledge and (depth of – [T]) research. However, we do not understand one aspect. After reading the article, one comes to the conclusion that horses, swords, bows and arrows etc. will be used in the war between (the Muslims comprising of – [T]) H̲ad̲rat Mahdî ﷺ and H̲ad̲rat ʿÎsâ ﷺ against the non-Muslims and Christians. The armies will face one another in the battlefield like the times of before.

You wrote that H̲ad̲rat Mahdî ﷺ will send nine horsemen from Constantinople to Shâm in order to find out about *Dajjâl*. It is as if there will be no aircraft. Then, H̲ad̲rat ʿÎsâ ﷺ will destroy *Dajjâl* using a spear. (Similarly, - [T]) when *Yâjûj* and *Mâjûj* will cause corruption, then they will have bows and arrows, i.e. it will not be the era of guns, rifles, pistols and explosives. From the time that man set foot on earth, science has always been developing and before *Qiyâmah,* it would have advanced in leaps (and bounds – [T]).

The second point is that you have written that upon the command of H̲ad̲rat ʿÎsâ ﷺ, a few individuals will take refuge in the fort of Mount T̲ûr in order to save themselves from the nation of *Yâjûj and Mâjûj*. This implies that the rest of the people who became Muslims will be left to the mercy of *Yâjûj and Mâjûj*. It is logical to assume that such a fort cannot accommodate so many people. I cannot remember a *duʿâ'* that I read in one book that Rasûlullâh ﷺ prescribed to recite for protection from *Dajjâl.*

[263] A newspaper published in Pakistan –[T]

Write this *du'â'* together with clarifying the above-mentioned points.

Answer:

The structure of civilization changes all the time. All would have suspected a person of being mad if he had to explain the communication systems and weapons that we have today, one hundred and fifty or two hundred years ago. Allâh knows best as to whether this scientific technology will advance or will it commit suicide and the structure of civilization would return to the like of former times.

The possibility of this second option always exists and the bodies of scientists tremble due to this. If this is the case, then no objection remains about the circumstances that will prevail during the era of Hadrat Mahdî ﵁ and Hadrat 'Îsâ ﵇.

We have been commanded to recite *Sûrah al Kahf* (the Cave) on Fridays. Every Muslim should recite at least the first and last ten verses. The following *du'â'* is narrated in the Ahâdîth,

اللهم إني أعوذبك من عذاب جهنم ، وأعوذبك من عذاب القبر ، وأعوذبك من فتنة المسيح الدجال . اللهم إني أعوذبك من فتنة المحيا والممات . اللهم إني أعوذبك من المأثم والمغرم . آپ کے مساءل اور ان کا حل ۱/۲۶۸،۲۶۹

O Allâh, verily I seek protection in You from the punishment of *Jahannam,* and I seek protection in You from the punishment of the grave, and I seek protection in You from the *fitnah* of *Al Masîh Ad Dajjâl.* O Allâh, verily I seek protection in You from the *fitnah* of life and death. O Allâh, verily I seek protection in You from sin and loss.[264]

Note: Some writers have referred to the equipment of war in the battles of H̲ad̲rat Mahdî ﵀ in new terms. From this, we understand that later inventions will also be used in his victories. This is only speculation. Allâh ﷻ knows best what is to happen.

PARTS OF THE INTERVIEW WITH H̲AD̲RAT MUFTÎ MUH̲AMMAD RAFÎ' 'UTHMÂNÎ *dâmat barakâtuhu*

Question:

Give us some guidance regarding the glad-tidings that Rasûlullâh ﷺ gave and provide an explanation that corroborates them.

Answer:

If we scrutinize the prophesies of Rasûlullâh ﷺ, then we learn that the politics, geography and the fast-changing conditions of the world are all taking the world to the time before the emergence of H̲ad̲rat Mahdî ﵀. This entire field is being prepared for it. It is also proven from the narrations that there will be great difference of opinion among the Muslims during the time of H̲ad̲rat Mahdî ﵀. He ﵀ will end the differences and the Islâmic *khilâfah* will once again be established. The head of this *khilâfah* will be H̲ad̲rat Mahdî ﵀. Apparently, this time does not seem far away.

Question:

---

264 Âp ke Masâ'il Aur un ka H̲al vol.1 pp.268-269

The emergence of *Dajjâl* is also said to concurrently occur with the emergence of H̲ad̲rat Mahdî ؓ?

Answer:
It will be a trying time for the entire *ummah*. It will not be a time of disgrace for the *ummah* because the Muslims will be united under the flag of one leader and the truth will be open before them. The decision of H̲ad̲rat Mahdî ؓ will stand as the truth and whatever is in conflict with it is baseless. They will not have the trouble we currently face, difficulty in deciding on who is correct. We acknowledge that many lives will be lost and great sacrifice will be given. However, there will not be wrangling and disgrace. Muslims will die honourably.[265]

Muftî Muh̲ammad Rafî' has written an article on this subject titled, *'Ambiyâ' kî sar Zamîn me Chand Roz'*. It was published in separate parts in *Al Balâgh*. The fifth part is indispensable in our study. He writes,
'Some signs of *Qiyâmah* are:
Most of the land stolen from the Muslims by the *Isrâ'îlîs* were seen together with the historical places we visited in Jordan. The hearts which have been wounded due to evil actions from before, when witnessing these places themselves, suffer injury upon injury. (Therefore, - [T]) we are suffering injury upon injury when looking at these events. If we look at the fast changing world and the way in which it is changing in the last sixty years, especially in the Middle East, in the light of the signs explained by Rasûlullâh ﷺ, then we clearly realize that the world is now moving rapidly towards *Qiyâmah*.

---

265 Al Balâgh vol.6 no.11, January 2004

At every step of the journey through Jordan and Syria, we see that the field for Imâm Mahdî's emergence and the war against Dajjâl is being prepared. (Similarly, - [T]) the killing of *Dajjâl* immediately after the descension of Hadrat 'Îsâ ﷺ during this battle as well as the mass killing of the Jews - which the Jews are unknowingly preparing themselves – is before us. Well before the time of Rasûlullâh ﷺ, Nebuchadnezzar defeated the Jews and they were dispersed all over the world in disgrace. This was their condition until approximately 60 years ago. Now, after thousands of years, they are coming from all parts of the world to Palestine. In other words, they are gathering at the place where they will be killed. They are making it apparent that they are busy in making the work of the army of Hadrat 'Îsâ ﷺ and Hadrat Mahdî ﷺ very easy. In the words of my honourable father[266], 'where will Hadrat 'Îsâ ﷺ go looking for them throughout the world?'

We learn that the Jews take *Dajjâl* to be their leader. What is surprising to note is that they are waiting for him at the place where he will come and be killed - in accordance to the prophesy of Rasûlullâh ﷺ. One of our hosts – Hasan Yûsuf, who was mentioned many times before – is from among the original residents of Palestine. He migrated from there approximately 25 to 30 years ago and is now living in 'Ammân. He told us that he went to a city called *'Ludd'* during a *tablîgh* journey to Palestine. This city is close to Jerusalem. He saw a big gate called *'Bâb Ludd'*[267]. The *Isrâ'îlî* administration wrote the following line on this gate,

---

[266] Muftî Muhammad Shafi' رحمه الله

[267] The door of Ludd

هنا يخرج ملك السلام

The king of peace *(Dajjâl)* will emerge here

Now, study a Hadîth in which Rasûlullâh ﷺ mentioned the details of the descent of Hadrat ʿÎsâ عليه السلام close to *Qiyâmah*. This Hadîth has been narrated through very authentic chains and three sahâbah ؓ and one mother of the believers – Hadrat ʿÂ'isha *radiyallâhu anha* - has narrated it. Rasûlullâh ﷺ said,

فيطلبه حتى يدركه بباب لد ، فيقتله . صحيح مسلم ، سنن أبو داؤد ، جامع ترمذي ، سنن ابن ماجة ، مسند أحمد

He will look for him until he finds him at Bâb Ludd. He will then kill him.[268]

We traveled in the vehicle of another one of our hosts - ʿAlî Hasan Ahmad al Bayârî, a famous businessperson of *Irbid* who is also linked to the effort of *tablîgh* – in the journey from ʿAmmân to *Irbid*. His father is also among the original residents of Palestine. In fact, he was a resident of this very *'Ludd'*. He migrated from there in 1948 and came here (to *Irbid*) – [T]). ʿAlî Hasan Ahmad al Bayârî was born here in 1951. Upon return from our tour, he hosted us in his magnificent house. In an enjoyable discussion, he narrated an incident of his. In 1980, he spent ten days in his hometown of *Ludd*. He said that there is a well at *Bâb Ludd*. The *Isrâʿîlî* administration wanted to destroy this well in order to make way for a road. However, bulldozers and other machinery could not destroy this well. They were forced to build the road around this well. Now, the following line is written there,

---

268 Sahîh Muslim, Sunan Abû Dâwûd, Jâmiʿ Tirmidhî, Sunan Ibn Mâjah, Musnad Ahmad

هذا مكان تاريخي

This is a historical site

This very ʿAlî H̲asan Ah̲mad al Bayârî told us of his cousin who has great interest in the signs of *Qiyâmah.* His cousin went to *Ludd.* He saw a palace there being built by the *Isrâ'îlîs* for their 'king of peace' *(Dajjâl).*

A WORTHY ACTION OF MAULÂNÂ RAFÎʿ UD DÎN رحمة الله عليه

H̲ad̲rat Maulânâ Rafîʿ ud Din رحمة الله عليه - the first principal of *Dar ul ʿUlûm* Deoband and a luminary of the *Naqshbandî* family - migrated to Makkah Mukarramah. He passed away there and is buried there too. He came to know of the H̲adîth in which it was mentioned that Rasûlullâh ﷺ gave the keys of the *Kaʿbah* to the *Shaybî* family. Therefore, even if all the families of Makkah Mukarramah were to be destroyed, the *Shaybî* family would survive until the Day of *Qiyâmah.*

Subsequently, Maulânâ Rafîʿ ud Dîn رحمة الله عليه thought of a strange plan of action. (He thought – [T]) that if this family is to remain until *Qiyâmah,* then they will definitely still be in existence during the era of the emergence of H̲ad̲rat Mahdî رضي الله عنه. When H̲ad̲rat Mahdî رضي الله عنه will emerge, then he will sit leaning against the *Kaʿbah* while the Muslims will pledge allegiance at his hands. The keys of the *Kaʿbah* will be with the *Shaybî* family. So, he took a small Qur'ân[269], a sword and wrote a letter addressed to <u>H</u>a<u>d</u>rat Mahdî ﷺ. The subject matter of the letter was as follows,

'The lowly one, Rafi' ud Dîn Deobandî is present in Makkah Mu'a<u>zz</u>amah. You are busy preparing for *jihâd*. You have such *mujahidîn* with you who will be rewarded like the *mujâhidîn* of Badr. This Qur'an is a gift to you from Rafi' ud Dîn and give this sword to one of the *mujâhidîn* so that he may participate in the battle on my behalf. I will thus be rewarded too.

I have given these three items to the *Shaybî* family and I have told them that your family will remain until *Qiyâmah*. This is a trust for the Mahdî ﷺ. When you pass away, then make a bequest to those who will replace you. Tell them to make the same bequest to those who will come after them. Every generation should make this bequest to the next until this trust reaches <u>H</u>a<u>d</u>rat Mahdî ﷺ.[270]

THE BEQUEST OF <u>H</u>A<u>D</u>RAT ABÛ HURAYRAH رضي الله عنه

عن أبي هريرة رضي الله عنه مرفوعا : ينزل عيسى بن مريم فيدق الصليب ، ويقتل الخنزير ويضع الجزية ، ويهلك الله عز وجل في زمانه الدجال ، وتقوم الكلمة لله رب العلمين – قال أبو هريرة رضي الله عنه : أفلا تروني شيخا كبيرا قد كادت أن تلتقي ترقوتاى من الكبر ، إني لأرجو أن لا أموت حتى ألقاه

---

269 The Urdu word has various translations. One of them is 'small Qur'an', another is 'a sword belt hung from the shoulders', and another is 'a necklace of flowers'. Allâh ﷻ knows best - [T]

270 Khu<u>t</u>bât <u>H</u>akîm ul Islâm vol.2 p.98

واحدثه عن رسول الله صلى الله عليه وسلم ويصدقه ، فـإن أنـا مـت قبـل أن ألقاه ولقيتموه بعدي فأقرأوا عليه مني السلام . السنن للداني ٢٤٢ رقم ٦٩١

It is narrated from Hadrat Abû Hurayrah ﷺ - in marfû ʿform – Îsâ bin Maryam will descend and he will break the cross, he will kill the pig and abrogate jizya. Allâh ﷻ will destroy Dajjâl in his time and the word of Allâh ﷻ will be established. Hadrat Abû Hurayrah ﷺ says, "Do you not find me advanced in age? My ribs are almost touching each other because of old age. It is my desire that my death does not come until I do not meet him (Hadrat Îsâ ﷺ) and I will narrate to him the Ahâdith of Rasûlullâh ﷺ and he will verify it. If I pass away before meeting him and you meet him, then give the message of my salâm to him."

DU'Â'

We stretch our hands in *du'â'* before Allâh ﷻ, asking Him to accept this work. May He make it a means of gaining the correct recognition of Hadrat Mahdî ؓ, and may He accept us to raise His word together with him (Hadrat Mahdî ؓ).

ربنا تقبل منا إنك أنت السميع العليم ، وتب علينا يا مولانا إنك أنت التواب الرحيم ، وصلى الله تعالى على خير خلقه سيدنا محمد وآله وصحبه وعلى من تبعهم بإحسان إلى يوم الدين . آمين

Mahmûd Sulaymân Hâfizjî (Bârdolî), Makkah Mukarramah – in whose precincts this pious servant (Hadrat Mahdî ؓ - [T]) will emerge in accordance to the glad-tidings of Rasûlullâh ﷺ.

BIBLIOGRAPHY

1. The Noble Qur'ân
2. Tafsîr Ibn Kathîr
3. Tafsîr At Tabarî
4. Hidâyat ul Qur'ân
5. As Sihâh As Sittah
6. Musnad Ahmad
7. Musnad Bazzâr
8. Musannaf ʿAbdur Razzâq
9. Musannaf Ibn Abî Shaybah
10. Sunan Ad Dâr Qutnî
11. Musnad Ash Shâmiyyîn
12. Mustadrak lil Hâkim
13. As Sunan lid Dânî
14. Dalâ'il un Nubuwwah
15. Fath al Bârî
16. ʿUmdatul Qârî
17. Fayd ul Bârî
18. Al Jâmiʿ Al Kabîr
19. Fayd al Qadîr
20. Fath al Mulhim
21. Takmila Fath al Mulhim
22. Ikmâl Ikmâl al Muʿlim
23. Mukammal al Ikmâl
24. Al Kaukab ad Durrî
25. Tuhfah al Ahwadhî
26. Al ʿArf ush Shadhî
27. Al ʿAun al Maʿbûd
28. Badhl al Majhûd
29. Misbâh uz Zujâjah

30. Ash'atul Lam'ât
31. Mirqât ul Mafâtîh
32. Kanz ul 'Ummâl
33. Muntakhab Kanz ul 'Ummâl
34. Al 'Arf al Wardî fî Akhbâr al Mahdî
35. 'Âridah al Ahwadhî
36. Al Bidâyah wa An Nihâyah
37. As Si'âyah
38. Al Mughnî li Ad Dhahabî
39. Tahdhîb ut Tahdhîb
40. At Tadhkirah lil Qurtubî
41. At Târîkh li Ibn 'Asâkir
42. Al Ahâdîth Ad Da'îfah lish Shaukânî
43. Silsilah Al Ahâdîth Ad Da'îfah
44. Al Kâmil fî Du'afâ' Ar Rijâl li Ibn 'Adî
45. Nukhba al La'âlî sharh Bad' ul Amâlî
46. Al Manâr al Munîf li Ibn Al Qayyîm
47. Mîzân al I'tidâl
48. Kifâyatul Muftî
49. Fatâwâ Mahmûdiyya
50. Fatâwâ Rahîmiyya
51. Khayr al Fatâwâ
52. Al Hâwî lil Fatâwâ
53. Nawâdir ul Fiqh
54. Izâlatul Khifâ'
55. Tuhfa e Khilâfat of Maulânâ 'Abd ush Shakûr Lakhnawî
56. Târîkh ul Khulafâ'
57. Ma'ârif ul Hadîth
58. Majma' Bihâr al Anwâr
59. Tarjumân us Sunnah

60. Rahmatullâh al Wâsiʿa
61. Al Mahdî wal Masîh of Muftî Yûsuf Ludhiyânwî رحمة الله عليه
62. Lisân ul Mîzân
63. Al Ishâʿa li Ashrât As Sâʿa
64. Sharh Al Fiqh Al Akbar
65. Sharh ʿAqîdah As Safârînî
66. An Nibrâs
67. ʿAqîdah Zuhûr e Mahdî
68. Arwâh e Thalâtha
69. Imâm Mahdî, Shakhsiyyat wa Haqîqat
70. Imâm Mahdî of Maulânâ Diyâ ur Rahmân Fârûqî رحمة الله عليه
71. Imâm Mahdî ka Zuhûr Nahî Huwa Muftî Salmân Mansûrpûrî
72. Nuzûl ʿÎsâ Zuhûr e Masîh of Maulânâ Idrîs Kândehlawî رحمة الله عليه
73. ʿAqâ'id e Islâm of Maulânâ Muhammad Pâlan Haqqânî رحمة الله عليه
74. Kitâb al Fitan wa Ashrât us Sâʿa of ʿAllâah Dânî رحمة الله عليه
75. ʿAlâmât e Qiyâmah of Muftî Rafiʿ ʿUthmânî
76. Kitâb ul Fitan of Nuʿaym bin Hammâd رحمة الله عليه
77. ʿAlâmât e Qiyâmah of Shâh Rafiʿ ud Dîn رحمة الله عليه
78. Jawâhir ul Îmân
79. Jawâhir ul Fiqh
80. ʿAqâ'id e Islâm of Maulânâ Muhammad Idrîs Kândehlawî رحمة الله عليه
81. Radd e Qâdiyâniyyat ke Zarî Usûl
82. Fiqhî Jawâhir
83. Malfuzât e Faqîh ul Ummah
84. An Nihâyah li Ibn Kathîr
85. Khutbât Hakîm ul Islâm
86. Âp ke Masâ'il aur un ka Hal

Notes

Notes

مفاتيح الفرج

Keys to Success

For the Satisfaction of the Heart and Removal of Difficulties

Translation of the Famous Book:
"MAFATIHUL FARJ"

By: Qari Muhammad Siddiq Manshawi Sahib
رحمہ اللہ تعالیٰ

Jointly Published by:
Zam Zam Publishers
and
Madrasah Arabia Islamia

Family Ties

Miscellaneous Advices Regarding the Fostering and Maintaining of Family Ties

Jointly Published by:
Zam Zam Publishers
and
Madrasah Arabia Islamia

Summary of the Qur'ân Majîd

By:

Hadrat Maulânâ Aslam Shaikûpûrî Sâhib

(دامت برکاتهم)

Translated by:
Maulânâ Moosa Kajee

Translation edited by
Maulânâ Ahmed Hansa

Jointly Published by:
Zam Zam Publishers
and
Madrasah Arabia Islamia

AN ECHO
FROM
THE HEART

A collection of lectures
delivered by:

Hadrat Maulānā ʿAbdullāh Sāhib Kāpaudrī
(former rector of Dar al-Ulum Falah-e-Darain, Tadkeshwar)

Translated by:

Moulānā Mahomed Mahomedy

Jointly Published by:
Zam Zam Publishers
and
Madrasah Arabia Islamia